TOO SOON TO SAY GOODBYE

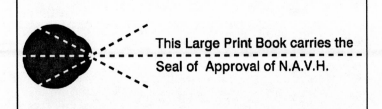

This Large Print Book carries the
Seal of Approval of N.A.V.H.

Too Soon to Say Goodbye

Art Buchwald

THORNDIKE PRESS

An imprint of Thomson Gale, a part of The Thomson Corporation

THOMSON

GALE

Detroit • New York • San Francisco • New Haven, Conn. • Waterville, Maine • London

THOMSON

GALE

LIBRARY OF CONGRESS CATALOGING-IN-PUBLICATION DATA

Buchwald, Art.
    Too soon to say goodbye / by Art Buchwald.
        p. cm. — (Thorndike Press large print biography)
    ISBN-13: 978-0-7862-9407-7 (hardcover : alk. paper)
    ISBN-10: 0-7862-9407-8 (hardcover : alk. paper)
    1. Buchwald, Art. 2. Humorists, American — 20th century — Biography.
3. Large type books. I. Title.
PS3503.U1828Z46 2007
814'.54—dc22
[B]   2006101814

Published in 2007 by arrangement with Random House, Inc.

Printed in the United States of America on permanent paper
10 9 8 7 6 5 4 3

What started out the worst of times ended up the best of times.

The big news of 2006 is that I'm still alive. After being in the hospice waiting to die, I said, "To hell with it, I'm going to write a book."

This is how it worked. I sat in my hospice chair and I dictated everything to my associate, Cathy Crary, who sat there in the living room with her computer. She not only took down my dictation but she also laughed when she was supposed to and made it possible for me to write. I am grateful to her and always will be.

July 2006

CONTENTS

1
ON STANDBY FOR HEAVEN

I am in a hospice and I have this recurring dream. I am at Dulles airport and I have a reservation to go to heaven. I go into the terminal and look at the list of flights. Heaven is at the last gate.

I don't know if they have reading material on the plane, so I stop at the magazine stand and pick up *Vanity Fair, The New Yorker,* and *Playboy.* I also buy a package of gum and some M&M's. Then I head toward security.

I have bought my ticket, which says, "When you go to heaven, you need only one bag, but do not include a cigarette lighter or sharp scissors." I stand in line for hours. I didn't realize how many people were on the same flight.

I run into several friends, and I am surprised to see them. They hadn't mentioned they were going too. In my dream several of them are younger than I am, and I know two who were smokers.

I finally get to the security gate, holding on to my bag for dear life.

The agent says, "You don't have to bring your computer with you. They have them up there."

I say to the agent, "I want to hold on to my bag because I don't want you people to lose it."

Then they make me take off my jacket, my belt, and my shoes.

When I ask why, the agent says, "You don't want to wear shoes in heaven. They scratch up the floor."

They send me through another gate because I have a pacemaker. Then they make me stick out my arms and they scan my legs with a wand.

I finally get to the departure gate. Dulles is crowded. In my dream, there are no seats in the waiting area, so I go to Starbucks to kill time. I am not sure if you get lunch on the plane to heaven. For all I know, they give you a bagel and cream cheese and a soft drink. I am warned by an attendant that I can't get out of my seat on the flight.

This is kind of silly, because who would hijack a plane to heaven?

It's open seating on the plane. I know heaven is a wonderful place, but on the way there you have to sit three across. As with all flights, there are emergency exits in case the pilot changes his mind. There are also life jackets under each seat. In my dream the flight attendants are very beautiful, and they hand out blankets and pillows.

I enter the waiting area. The loudspeaker says, "Heaven is at the last gate. There will be intermediate stops in Dallas, Chicago, and Albuquerque. The plane has just arrived."

I go up to the desk and ask, "Am I entitled to frequent flyer miles?"

The agent says, "You won't need any, because you're not coming back."

Now, this is the part I love. (Remember, this is *my* dream.) The loudspeaker says, "Because of inclement weather, today's flight to heaven has been canceled. You can come back tomorrow and we'll put you on standby."

2
THE MAN WHO
WOULD NOT DIE

By all rights this book never should have been written. By all rights, I should be dead.

And thereby hangs the tale.

I am writing this book from a hospice. But being in the hospice didn't work out exactly the way I had expected. By all rights I should have finished my time here in mid-March 2006 — at least, that's when Medicare stopped paying.

What happened to get me to the hospice was this: I was riding the elevator up to my room at the acute care facility when I saw a sign that said there was also a hospice in the building. At that point, all I knew about hospices was that they cared for terminally ill patients. I arranged a tour of the hospice and everything looked very good to me.

At that moment, I decided I wanted to come here. I had lost a leg at Georgetown University Hospital. I missed my leg, but when they told me I would also have to take dialysis for the rest of my life, I decided — too much.

My decision coincided with my appearance on Diane Rehm's radio talk show, which has over a million listeners. I talked with her from the hospice about my decision not to take dialysis. It is one thing to choose to go into a hospice; it's another thing to get on the air and tell everybody about it.

The listener response was very much in my favor. Later, I received more than 150 letters, and most of them said I was doing the right thing. This, of course, made me feel good. I wrote back to them: "As Frank Sinatra would say, 'I did it my way.' "

When I entered the hospice I was under the impression it would be a two- or three-week stay. But I was wrong. Every day I sit in a beautiful living room where I can have anything I want; I can even send out to McDonald's for milkshakes and hamburgers. Most people have to watch their diets. No one can believe that I can eat anything I want.

I have a constant flow of visitors. Many of them have famous names, and my family is impressed with who shows up. (I suspect I would not be getting the same attention if I were on dialysis.) I hold court in the big living room. We sit here for hours talking about the past, and since it's my show, we talk about anything that comes to my mind. It's a wonderful place, and if for some reason somebody forgets to come see me, there's always television and movies on DVD.

I keep checking with the nurses and doctors about when I'm supposed to take the big sleep. No one has an answer. One doctor says, "It's up to you." And I say, "That's a typical doctor's answer."

I receive plates and baskets of delicious food: home-cooked meals, treats from the delicatessen, frozen yogurt from Häagen-Dazs.

Everybody wants to please me. Food seems to be very important, not only to my guests, but also to me. If they bring food, they get even better treatment from me. One day I told a friend I had dreamed the night before of a corned beef sandwich. The next day I got ten.

When my friend Ira Harris heard that another friend, Herb Siegel, had sent me a cheesecake, he said Herb didn't know anything about cheesecake because he's from New York, and he would send me a Chicago cheesecake. To prove his point, Ira sent several giant cheesecakes. (I'm not sure I still like cheesecake.)

Also, I have received dozens of flower arrangements. People don't send roses when you are on dialysis.

I don't know if this is true or not, but I think some people, not many, are starting to wonder why I'm still around. In fact, a few are sending me get-well cards. They must have been purchased by my friends' secretaries. These are the hard ones to answer.

So far things are going my way. I am known in the hospice as "The Man Who Would Not Die." How long they allow me to stay here is another problem. I don't know where I'd go now, or if people would still want to see me if I weren't in a hospice. But in case you're wondering, I'm having a swell time — the best time of my life.

Dying isn't hard. Getting paid by Medicare is.

3
How I Wound Up
in a Hospice

To explain how I landed here, I have to go back to September 28, 2005, when I was feeling fine and celebrating my eightieth birthday at the French embassy in Washington, D.C. It was a gala affair attended by four hundred people, and it was a fundraiser for the Brady Center to Prevent Gun Violence. I remember saying at the time:

> Becoming eighty is a matter of life or death. I chose life. It is a much better position to be in, and it is easier on your back.
> You don't become eighty all by yourself. There are many people out there tonight who helped me along the way. First, my sisters, Edith, Doris, and Alice; and then my wife, Ann, who was my inspiration; and my children, whom I love dearly. Finally, there is Dr. Michael Newman, who has taken care of me for twenty-five years and made sure I could be here tonight.

I haven't forgotten my friends, those who are celebrating with me tonight, and those who couldn't be here but will always be in my memory book.

I also haven't forgotten the grudges I've carried throughout my lifetime. They make me feel warm inside. The ones I have never gotten over are the hurts of my childhood. Then, when I grew up, I held a grudge against Eddie Murphy and Paramount for lifting my idea for *Coming to America.* And the big one: After fifty years, *The New York Times* dropped my column from the *International Herald Tribune.*

At a certain time in life — actually, right now — the two questions that become uppermost in my mind are "What am I doing here?" and "Where am I going?"

The first answer is a narcissistic one. I was put on earth to make people laugh. The second one is much harder — I have no idea where I am going and no one else knows. And if they claim they know, they don't know what the hell they are talking about.

I did not know at the time how smart I was then, to be talking about where I'm going.

Declining Dialysis

I first became acquainted with my kidneys twenty years ago. All my life I had just assumed they would not give me any problems. The kidney does its duty discreetly and without fanfare.

For thousands of years it has been the most underrated organ in the human body. Sonnets, love songs, and masterpieces of fiction have been devoted to the heart, yet if it were not for the kidneys working day and night to excrete poisons from our systems, the heart would not have a chance.

Men and women cannot live by bread alone. They must also tinkle. Show me someone who has no trouble tinkling and I will show you a happy and rich person.

I started paying attention to my kidneys when I attempted to pass a kidney stone some years ago in Evansville, Indiana. It was an experience I still haven't forgotten. The only way to describe it is to imagine trying to push the Rock of Gibraltar through the Suez Canal.

When someone is climbing the walls trying to eliminate the stone, he will promise anything to get relief. He would give all his worldly possessions for one shot of Demerol.

I discovered at that moment that people

in Washington do not understand how the kidney functions. For example, when a reporter in Washington says he's going to "take a leak," he usually means he's going to pick up a top-secret document from some high government official.

Because I had my attack in Evansville, Indiana, the AP wire sent out four paragraphs on the stone. It became famous all over the world, so much so that I received a letter from the United States Geological Survey in Reston, Virginia. These are the folks who study moon rocks.

When I returned to Washington, the geologists offered to study my kidney stone. They called it Project Buchwald Stone.

Dr. Michael Rubin scoffed at the size of the Buchwald Stone. He said he had passed stones ten times larger, and he wondered if I was just a professional whiner.

Dr. Wornick, who studied my stone, was more sympathetic. He proved on the blackboard that size was not the main factor in a kidney stone's pain. The amount of anguish and screaming was in direct proportion not to the size of the stone, but to the length of the path the stone had traveled.

This probably destroyed Dr. Rubin's chance of winning the Nobel Prize.

Once the report was in on the Buchwald

Stone, they suggested constructing a building to house it, so people could come view it. It would be an attraction, like the Dead Sea Scrolls.

It's amazing how many ideas you can conjure up as a solution to your problems. The first thought I had, as do most people with kidney problems, was "Where can I get a transplant?" I discovered that people line up — sometimes for years — waiting for a kidney. One of my best friends, Erma Bombeck, waited a long time, but it was a little late by the time she got a new one.

My doctor said that even if I got in line for a transplant it wouldn't help me. I'm not a good candidate because of my age, and blood pressure. Plus, the drugs necessary to prevent rejection are risky for someone my age.

My daughter-in-law Tamara offered to give me one of her kidneys.

I, of course, refused. There is something strange about walking around with your daughter-in-law's kidney.

Dialysis is like being connected to a washing machine so that all the by-products (toxins and other metabolic waste) are removed by a blood filtration machine. This means washing out all the toxins three times a week, for five hours at a time.

I didn't think my kidneys would let me down, given our long relationship. But in fact they steadily declined, and my doctors told me again that dialysis would soon be necessary. I got mad at my kidneys because I had treated them very well. And this was the gratitude they gave me? Eventually I agreed to dialysis, but I had a counteroffer: Could it wait until after the summer?

So that was the plan.

Then, a few weeks after my wonderful eightieth birthday party, I experienced a sudden onset of terrible pain in my right foot. I called my doctor, Michael Newman, who still makes house calls. He looked at my foot and said that I probably had some blood clots in the arteries of my foot, blocking circulation. He said this was an emergency.

Dr. Newman drove me to Georgetown University Hospital. There the doctors tried very hard to dissolve the clots and restore circulation, but it was not successful. I would lose my foot and part of my leg! I was not happy to hear this. Dr. Newman said that if I didn't have the operation, my situation was terminal. If I didn't have my leg removed, I would die of gangrene — a slow and painful death. That didn't sound very pleasant.

As it turned out, the dye used to perform the angiogram added insult to injury: My failing kidneys had now totally failed. My doctors told me I would need to begin dialysis immediately so as to make it possible to proceed with the amputation.

Talk about a double whammy. I was upset, angry, and depressed about what was happening to me. I was not sure I wanted any part of it.

Still, I agreed to begin dialysis so that my foot and lower leg could be amputated. After surgery, I agreed to continue dialysis, as I was not getting much support from my loved ones for the dying option, which I personally thought was best. I tried dialysis twelve times and decided I didn't like it. "That's it," I said. "I don't see a future in this and I don't want to do it anymore!" I had discovered the idea of the hospice by then, and knew I had an alternative.

Dr. Newman said, "It's your choice. You're the only one who can decide." I knew the entire family was against the idea of stopping dialysis. Everybody warned me that I was signing my own death certificate. Without dialysis I would last only a couple of weeks. I realized that by throwing in the towel I would hurt a lot of people, particularly my children, Jennifer, Joel, and Connie. There was tremendous pressure to take dialysis, and there were lots of tears when I broke the news to the family that I was not going to do it.

Dr. Newman arranged for me to be transferred here to the hospice. It's a nice place, but it's not easy to get into. It was like applying to Harvard.

No one gave me a clear idea about what might happen here, and no one mentioned that my condition might actually improve.

4
LIFE AT THE HOSPICE

On February 7 I was given a room at the Washington Home and Hospice. By this time I figured that with any luck I might be around for three weeks.

The hospice is on Upton Street in northwest Washington, D.C. It's a busy street, and as I like to tell my visitors, "Dying is easy; parking is impossible."

This hospice has fourteen beds. The average stay here before you go to heaven is a few days to two weeks. If you are going downhill, Medicare pays for it. If your condition stays the same as when you arrived, Medicare will not pick up the tab.

The purpose of hospice is to let you go with dignity and make death easier on you and your family. The first hospice was founded in England in 1967 by physician Dame Cicely Saunders. Dr. Saunders introduced the program to the United States, and the first hospice was established in

Connecticut in 1974. Besides residential hospice, the program also works with people who choose to die in their own homes.

My hospice in Washington, D.C., has a large sitting area for families, which I now call my salon. I spend each day in my salon, greeting friends, watching television, reading, and taking naps. At night I return to my bedroom. It's very rare that patients ever come out of their bedrooms to the living area. Most of them are too sick.

The family area is quite comfortable, with couches, tables, a library, a full kitchen, and a play area with toys for children. The biggest attraction is a large aquarium.

Families come here to pray, console one another, and wait. A large picture window runs the length of one wall, overlooking a beautiful garden with flowers, trees, and a fountain. People can go out there to find peace and quiet.

While I was sitting in my salon one day, an elderly gentleman came up to me to say he had just brought his wife in, and she was now in one of the rooms. He said they'd been married for sixty-six years. I sympathized with his plight. That afternoon he came back to say his wife had died.

On another afternoon, a lady brought her

father to the hospice and told me in the course of our conversation that she was an assistant director at the zoo in charge of the panda house. By luck, my grandchildren were visiting, and I introduced them. She promised they could come any time to see the pandas.

Large families frequently come to the hospice. A twenty-five-year-old woman was dying of AIDS. Her mother, the children, and all of her relatives sat in the living room for a vigil.

Another time, I was watching television and a family had gathered in the far corner of the room. One of the nurses came up and said to me, "Could you please turn the television down, because they just lost their father and they're praying."

The family room is where I hold court and where I said goodbye to people before I realized I wasn't going anywhere just yet. I also use the couch for therapy sessions with my friends.

They will start by talking about my problems, but then switch immediately and start telling me about theirs. I only charge $75 an hour, because after all, you don't want to make money in a hospice.

Unless they've had some experience with it,

the hospice is still a mystery to most people. Because hospice deals with death, people tend not to talk about it.

I maintained everyone has to die — I still do. The hospice gives a person the opportunity to die with dignity. It provides care, help, and as much comfort as possible. The circumstances of people finding out about my being in a hospice made everyone feel empathy toward my situation.

Because I've stayed around a lot longer than I was supposed to, I've had a chance to see all my friends, and also to speak with them on the phone. At first everybody came here to say goodbye. But time kept ticking by, and at four months in, my kidneys were still working. It is a mystery to my doctors, and my friends claim it is a miracle.

I've been here so long that I've decided the living room is a shrine. I tell people if they come here I will cure them of all their illnesses, the way they do at Lourdes.

Media Star for Death

It was after I'd been in the hospice for two weeks that I became a media star by accident, by going on Diane Rehm's radio show. I figured, what the heck, I had nothing else to do. I went on and talked about hospice, about not taking dialysis, and about what it was like to die. I had a feeling Diane's listeners would want to know what I had told my children, and I discussed how they were reacting to my decision. The interview produced 150 letters and e-mails, the majority of which were sympathetic.

Diane made me into a celebrity — the only person who became famous for dying. People decided I was a hero. You accept every compliment you can get when you're in a hospice.

After Diane Rehm, television producers and editors thought there was a story here: "Man refuses dialysis, chooses death." From then on the media heavyweights decided they had a character who was willing to die and talk about it.

First there was *This Week* with George Stephanopoulos. And then, hallelujah, Sharon Waxman wrote a long piece about me in the Sunday *New York Times.* As you know, you have never actually existed unless you have been written about in *The New York Times.* Usually you have to settle for an obituary, but this was a feature.

After that, Joe Brown interviewed me for Jim Lehrer's *NewsHour.* I appeared on CNN, on Channel 7 with Gordon Peterson, in *The Washington Post,* and on the front page of *USA Today.* Then Tom Brokaw asked me to be on the *Today* show.

Chris Wallace interviewed me for *Fox News Sunday.* Chris maintained that becoming a hospice patient was a good career move.

I enjoyed the interviews because it gave me something to do besides watch *Wheel of Fortune.*

5
CAREGIVERS

The godmother of the hospice is Chris Turner. She is in charge of twenty-five employees, including all the nurses, nurse's assistants, social workers, and volunteers. She oversees the care of the three hundred or so people who come into and go from the hospice each year.

We have had a special relationship because her husband is a major in the Marine Corps. I found out after several weeks that she's tougher than he is.

I asked Chris, "What do we know about hospice?"

She said, "Hospice is the true art of nursing care. It is nurses one on one with patients, giving them care and comfort at the end of life. It is like the priesthood in that there is a calling."

When the patient enters the hospice, an entire team sets to work to meet the family's needs — a doctor, a team of nurses, a case manager, a social worker, a chaplain, a nursing assistant, a bereavement coordinator, and of course, the volunteers.

The social worker is there to assist with everything having to do with coming into the hospice. In a hospice, the family members are as important as the patient, and most of the support from the social worker goes to the family, who are on an emotional roller coaster. The social worker is an advocate, a mediator, and a bereavement counselor. The social worker must speak the many "languages" of people from different cultures and socioeconomic backgrounds. Put simply, the social worker helps families prepare for death.

The hospice volunteers play a vital role. Many first learned about the hospice program when a family member or loved one received hospice care. They too are drawn by a desire to comfort those at the end of their lives. Some volunteers see the work as a way of confronting their own mortality.

In my hospice the volunteers answer the phones and screen the calls, which frees up the nurses to spend more time with patients. They also run errands for families and staff members.

One of the volunteers told me, "The cream of volunteering is contact with patients, and being able to communicate to them that another person cares about their dying." He said one of the most gratifying moments he had experienced was when a patient said, just before dying, "Thank you for caring."

Another volunteer told me that dying people seem to fall into two categories. One group was at peace and said, "I want to go home," which meant heaven. The other group she saw were people who said, "I have to get up and do something," or "I have to go somewhere." They had unfinished business.

Chris is in charge of which patients are accepted into the hospice. It is harder than getting into MIT. You have to have a certificate from a doctor that you have less than six months to live.

I asked her, "Can children come to the hospice to visit their loved one?"

She said, "Yes, it helps them and the patients very much. When they come here we work with all the members of the family who are affected by the death. Sometimes the adults don't want children to be aware that their loved one is no longer going to be with them.

"What I love to see after someone dies is

twenty people showing up. They order pizza and celebrate the person's life."

I said to Chris, "You hire all the people, the nurses, the aides, etcetera. What do you look for?"

She said, "These are people who should be able to deal with death and have a feeling they are making an important contribution to the last chapter of a person's life."

Dr. Matt Kestenbaum, the medical director, told me, "People don't understand the medical role in hospice. We're not here to pull the plug. We let nature take its course and we give patients all the things they need to be comfortable. If there is one phrase to describe what we do, it is, trying to avoid as much pain as possible. This applies not only in the residential hospice, but also to the care we provide in a patient's home."

The staff members of my hospice come from countries all around the world. My doctor, Cecilia Chukwu, is from Nigeria, as is one of the nurses. There are two nurses from Korea, one from Ghana, one from Barbados, and one from the Ivory Coast. There are also several American nurses. They all do everything for me, including attaching and detaching my new leg.

Nurse Jackie Lindsey is my "Chief Ball Breaker." She gives me a bath every morning, and dresses me so she won't be ashamed of me when I'm sitting in the salon. Imagine, if you will, that you are a man who can't bathe himself. The person who does it wants you to be clean.

I told her once, "That's no fun."

Her reply was, "Someone has to do it."

Then I asked her if she gets attached to her patients.

She said, "Some I do, particularly if I become their confidant and they tell me things they would not tell anyone else. I've found it's harder for the family of the patient to accept what's happening. In most cases — not all — the dying person has accepted his fate."

I asked Jackie if when she goes home at night she thinks about the people she takes care of.

She said, "Sometimes I do. The ones that affect me the most are young people from twenty to forty. I have to come to terms with it. Of course I feel sad."

I asked Jackie how she could do this type of work for so long.

She said, "I have taken care of three thousand people over thirty-seven years — some for several days, some for weeks, and, as in your case, some for months. I consider dying a very important part of life. I feel good in the sense that since these people are in pain, and most of them don't have very long to live, I can make their journey easier."

"When you're taking care of people who are dying, does it help to have a belief in God?"

She said, "Yes, I believe that God is there and wants me to help."

Jackie is the mother I never had. She gives me hope, love, and encouragement. She listens to all my stories and I listen to all of hers.

Finally I asked her, "Don't you feel bad when you hit my family jewels?"

"No," she replied, "because when I do it, I always say I'm sorry."

6
THE QUESTION OF DEATH

I am constantly asked the questions "What is death?" and "Have you seen it?"

Many of us have seen someone die — or have even had a near-death experience ourselves. Because of my situation, people consider me an expert.

I had been lying in the hospice for two months with nothing better to do when I decided to start my column up again. People saw the column reappear in *The Washington Post* and began asking questions. "If he's about to die, what's he writing a column for?"

This led to many discussions on the subject of death — where people were going after they die, who makes the decision to die, and how much time we have left before the fatal moment.

If I'd had a heart attack, I might not have had time to say goodbye to anybody or even take care of my personal affairs. A heart attack is unpredictable.

On the other hand, cancer can be a long-term illness — ranging from a month to a year. People waste away, and there's a lot of sadness in seeing somebody you love suffer this way.

In my case, I had failing kidneys, so my death was supposed to be not too fast, and not too slow, but just right.

The nurses in the hospice had told my family that death was imminent. They obviously didn't say it around me, but they discussed it with my family and among themselves.

As time went on, I became the star patient at the hospice, because I didn't go according to their plan. Against the odds, my kidneys started working again and could function without dialysis. The employees showed me off to prospective patients and their families. I became the hospice poster boy, and being the ham I am, I enjoyed it.

Hospices have never gotten much attention, because people connect them with death. People are afraid of the mystery of death. Relatives and friends are initially afraid to visit. It's a totally new ballgame.

Of course people want to talk about death, if you give them permission. I always give people permission to discuss it. I discovered it made them very happy to be able to share fears and questions about dying.

To quote Hamlet, "To be or not to be — that is a very good question."

The Afterlife

People often ask me if there is an afterlife. I answer them by saying, "If I knew, I would tell you."

This does not mean that everyone knows more than I do on the subject, including priests (Christian or Hindu), rabbis, or imams. I haven't yet made up my mind which one of these groups has the answer, but the nice thing about a hospice is we can talk about death openly. Most people are afraid that if they even mention it, they will bring bad karma on themselves.

I spoke to a Catholic who questioned the idea that I am not certain where I will go after life. This person couldn't believe that I didn't know, and said, "Aren't you going to meet in the hereafter all those people you used to know in life?" I'm still not so sure.

People talk about heaven as the place where we are all going to wind up. The problem with thinking about heaven is that you also have to think about hell. The irony of our culture is that people are constantly telling other people to go to hell, but no one tells them to go to heaven.

A friend of mine, Larry Gelbart, said he thinks the end will come for most people when all the phone companies merge and there is only one company left.

One joker said he thought the only person who knows for a fact that there is a hereafter is Pat Robertson of *The 700 Club*. When he was asked how Robertson would know, his answer was, "He's got the largest TV audience, and he wouldn't be allowed to say it if it wasn't true." Maybe the only people who will go to Robertson's heaven are those who contribute to his church.

I'm not denying it's possible that heaven truly exists. If it makes someone happy to believe in heaven, that's wonderful.

Some of my guests at the hospice maintain they have actually talked to people who have died. Every person has a different story. Some say they nearly died. Others have been in the room when a person passed away. None of my visitors talked about ghosts, though.

I don't doubt what they say. What's beautiful about death is you can say anything you want to, as long as you don't lord it over others, pretending to know something they don't.

The thing that is very important, and why I'm writing this book, is that whether they like it or not, everyone is going to go. The big question we still have to ask is not where we're going, but what we were doing here in the first place.

Thinking About Heaven

People like to ask me deep questions. One day my friend Morgan asked, "Is there a class system in heaven?"

I said, "You mean rich people and poor people?"

He said, "That's right."

I replied, "It's very possible, because rich people have built all the churches, synagogues, and mosques. Poor people don't have enough money even to fill in a stained glass window."

Morgan said, "I thought as much. Rich people probably have the best hotel rooms, and the most exclusive golfing clubs."

I said, "It could be. Poor people can always caddy for the rich people."

Morgan asked, "Is there a dress code in heaven? Will the rich people still wear Dior, Gucci, and Chanel?"

I said, "Yes, because your status in heaven will be based on how beautiful you look and how much Botox you can afford. But, now,

Morgan, this is just conjecture. There is a possibility that everyone in heaven will be wearing the same clothes from JCPenney and Macy's. This might tick the rich people off. I am certain they have it in their minds that their way of life will continue in heaven. I'm just guessing this, but if they can't be rich in heaven, they might not want to go there."

Morgan asked, "What about automobiles? Will the rich have Mercedeses and Lexuses and the poor drive around in used Chevrolets?"

"Yes, that's the way it will be, provided they have highways there. And there is no speed limit."

Morgan asked, "And private airplanes?"

"The affluent demand them as their right."

Morgan asked, "When you get to heaven and you're poor, can you work your way up to being rich?"

I said, "Yes, that's known as the Heavenly Dream. I heard of one man who arrived as a pizza delivery guy. In just a year he had Pizza Huts all over the sky. I guess everybody wants to know if it's even possible to be rich or poor in heaven. If you thought there was a chance you might be poor in heaven, you might not make a big effort to

41

get there."

Morgan said, "I read in one paper that real estate is getting very expensive in heaven. A few years ago a golden castle in the sky went for ten million. Now you can't even touch it for twenty-five. What about taxes?"

I replied, "As far as I know, there are no taxes. That's why it's called heaven."

"That means there are no H&R Block stores up there."

"Nope. There isn't even an IRS."

"That's the best thing I've heard about heaven so far."

I said, "Paying taxes is hell. Morgan, I would be a fraud if I said I knew exactly what went on in heaven. I'd like to be a rich man when I go there. You can afford to go to the opera and get better tables in the restaurants. And the beauty of it all is there is no tipping. If everybody were the same, heaven would be a socialist state, and you wouldn't want to belong to that, would you?"

Meet the Devil

Long before I knew about death, I had already learned about the devil.

When I was about three years old I had rickets, so my father sent my sister Doris and me to stay in a private home in Flushing, New York, with mother-and-daughter nurses. They were a pair of Seventh Day Adventists, so they had more than a nodding acquaintance with the devil.

The nurses warned that if we ate fish or meat, or even eggs, then the devil would pounce on us. If we went to the movies, listened to pop music, or enjoyed other forms of entertainment, the devil would take us straight to hell.

We went to church every Saturday and prayed to God that the devil wouldn't find us.

By the way, he didn't look like the devil drawn by most artists, with a pitchfork and horns. My devil was a gray ghost with a face like the vicious dog next door that barked every time I came near his fence.

Once the idea of the devil was implanted in my mind, it never left. I thought he was watching me all the time. Let me say, it was a frightening childhood.

Everyone carries the fears of childhood into adulthood. I now eat fish and meat under duress. I watch movies and listen to jazz and don't go to church. But there is something in me that still says I am sinning.

When I was having sex, the devil was always at the end of my bed, muttering

"Sinful, sinful, sinful."

The nurses at the private home in Flushing told me that the devil and God were at war. God was stern and unforgiving, they said. Nevertheless, as a child I prayed to Him every night. If I needed a favor, I would ask Him for one.

I recall once I lost ten cents, which I had wrapped in a handkerchief intending to buy a loaf of bread. I said, "God, God, help me find it. I'll do anything if you tell me where it is." He didn't tell me, and I decided the devil must have found it before I did. (Though I couldn't figure out what he would do with bread.)

I also talked to Him when I didn't do my homework, or after I fell while roller skating.

As time went on, I prayed to God less and less. I only became serious about getting His attention during World War II, when I was stationed on the Eniwetok Atoll as a Marine, loading bombs onto Corsair fighter airplanes. One night we had an air raid and the "fuckin' Japs" (a politically correct term in those days, before they sent us Hondas, Nissans, and Nikon cameras) bombed an ammunition dump next to our tent. I buried my head down in my foxhole and cried, "God, God, I don't want to die."

44

He must have heard me, because I am still alive.

In my youth, God was all-powerful and could do no wrong. But when I grew up I wasn't sure the God I was talking to was the right God. Everyone swears their own God is the only one, and if you pray to another you are an infidel, but I'm not too God-damned sure anymore.

I am Jewish, but I am not sure what kind of Jew I am. I know I can't handle the Orthodox Lord because there are too many rules to follow. Conservatives say there is an easier way, and they have fewer rules to obey; and the Reform Jews usually say their prayers in English.

Since the God factor plays such an important part in the hospice, I am still waiting for a sign to tell me which God is the real one.

I'm sure the devil is going to get mad when he reads this book.

7
DEPRESSION

Many people thought I was having or would have a depression when I lost my leg and entered the hospice. I was depressed, but that was nothing compared to the episodes I experienced in 1963 and 1987.

People ask, "Why would a funny man be depressed?"

My answer is, "Why not?"

Humorists (also people in show business, writers, and artists) are funny to cover up the hurts they have suffered as children. When the humor fails to work for them, they have a depression.

In 1997 Mike Wallace and I went public about our depression on *Larry King Live*. Larry had one of the highest ratings ever for that segment. After the show I called Larry and said, "You have the most depressed audience on television."

I heard from people then, just as I do now. Some were having a depression, some had experienced a depression, and some people had a depressed family member.

One lady said I saved her life. She had taken an overdose of pills, and my face came up on the television screen.

I was saying, "Don't hurt yourself. You will not only not be solving your problems, but you will be hurting the ones you love."

She said it was a sign and she went into the bathroom, stuck her finger down her throat, and whooped up her pills.

A few weeks after the show I was riding in a taxi in New York and the driver said, "Weren't you on the Larry King show talking about depression?"

I said I was the one.

"Do you take Prozac?"

"No," I said. "Do you?"

"I don't, but my dog does."

"How is he doing?" I asked.

"He is feeling much better."

Mike, Bill Styron, and I went around the country addressing mental health organizations. We received plaques and awards and became poster boys for mental illness. Now I have become the poster boy for death.

Tipper Gore gave me my favorite award at a reception in New York when she presented me with the "Lifetime Achievement

Award for Depression." It was given to me for my mantra, "Don't commit suicide, because you might change your mind two weeks later."

I had two serious depressions. I was told by Bill Styron that if I had one more I would be inducted into the "Bipolar Hall of Fame."

The price I paid for success was that by building a wall around me, no one could penetrate my real feelings. The scars of childhood were always there, and I was a fool to think I could get away with humor forever.

The worst thing about depression is the anger that goes with it. If you can turn the anger on somebody else, it is the first step in getting better. My depressions crept up on me. I was suicidal in both and had to go to the hospital in each case for weeks.

I couldn't believe what was happening to me. I was on a crying jag in the first depression and I was manic in the second.

In my manic phase I thought I could conquer the world. I could run from Eighty-ninth Street to Fifty-ninth Street in New York City in four minutes. I believed every woman was attracted to me. I gave my money away. I was on the greatest of highs.

No one recognized my manic phase because people thought I was being funny.

Then came the crash. I plunged into a terrible black inky lake. In this phase I was not only suicidal but also homicidal. I wanted to kill strangers passing me on the street. I broke out in a cold sweat and said, "I am not that kind of person." So I decided to kill myself.

My plan was to go to the Plaza, get a room on the sixteenth floor, and jump out the window. I spoke to my doctor on the phone and he said it wasn't such a good idea.

He talked me into coming back to Washington and he put me in the psychiatric ward of Georgetown University Hospital, where they fed me lithium.

A depression is impossible to describe to someone who hasn't had one. Even the psychiatrists who treat you for it don't know what they are talking about.

You are ashamed of yourself. You lose all self-respect. You feel worthless. You are sure everyone knows your dirty, dark secrets.

I had no energy. I was also paranoid. In my depression I didn't ask God to help me. I was sure that it was the devil's work and that I was already in hell and would never get out.

8
PEOPLE IN MY LIFE

Ann

My wife, Ann, died twelve years ago, and she was buried on Martha's Vineyard. That's where I'll be going — into the plot next to hers. We were married for forty years. It was a happy marriage, if you don't count the unhappiness. But at the end Ann had a heart attack and then lung cancer. She coped by turning her anger against me, to the point where I felt it best for both of us if I left home. Still, we remained very close. My son, Joel, took care of her as she suffered through a long illness. Finally on July 3, 1994, she passed away.

When a loved one dies, you carry around a lot of guilt. I still do. And even now, I hurt when I think about her. In an odd way, my days here in the hospice are somehow connected with her death. I think of her on Martha's Vineyard and dream that I'll be with her soon.

Several years ago I wrote a novel called *Stella in Heaven*. The main character in the story, Stella, dies and goes to heaven — heaven being the Ritz-Carlton in Florida. In heaven, Stella can have anything she wants. Her husband, Roger, is still on earth and Stella decides to start running his life, even to the point of trying to find another wife for him — but not seriously. Stella forms a search committee, but she winds up sabotaging Roger's relationships with every new woman he becomes interested in. The whole plot was based on how I felt after Ann died.

Of course, guilt is transferable; since I couldn't get rid of it, I carried it into my new relationships. Every time I saw something we had done together, I thought of Ann, whether it was walking down a street in Paris, going to the National Art Gallery in Washington, or seeing her pictures around the house.

Mother

I wasn't able to deal with my mother's death in the way most people do. She was taken away from me right after I was born and she spent the rest of her life in a mental hospital.

I never actually saw my mother. At the beginning it was because they wouldn't let

51

me, and at the end because I didn't want to. Growing up, my sisters had seen her in the hospital, but I never went. I could have when I became an adult, but I didn't want to. I was afraid she wouldn't know me, and that would destroy my fantasy of her.

Since I never knew her, I made up the mother I imagined she was. Over the years I kept a fantasy about "Mother." I realized I had no right to call her "Mom" because I didn't know her.

When my mother died, I wrote a eulogy based on what I thought she would have been like:

We gather here today to say farewell to Helen Kleinberger Buchwald. She was my mother. She was wise and beautiful and very caring.

Since I was her only boy she showered me with her love, but at the same time, she was strict when it came to my grades at school. She dreamed that I would become a doctor, a lawyer, or an accountant.

She always bought a new suit for me at Passover and, although she was Orthodox, she took me to the Christmas show at Radio City Music Hall. She had a beautiful voice and sang Hungarian songs and also melodies by Irving Berlin, who she said was the greatest songwriter in the world.

She always took my side in arguments with my sisters.

One night I slept with all my clothes on and she made me take them off in the morning. That evening, to punish me, she wouldn't give me any rice pudding, which was my favorite.

A psychiatrist told me that when you grieve you think of all the things you didn't do for your loved one and not the things you did do. I should have become a rabbi, which would have pleased my mother very much. I should have married a nice Jewish girl rather than a nice Catholic girl. When I left home I should have called her every day.

All of us in this synagogue regret the things we didn't do with Helen Kleinberger. She will be missed but not forgotten. I like to think she is now in heaven making rice pudding for the angels.

I never told anyone about my eulogy, but it always made me feel better.

Mother was in a state hospital for thirty-five years, having been diagnosed with manic depression. She died at age sixty-five.

I was in Europe at the time of my mother's death. My sisters didn't call or telegraph me. They wrote me a letter that arrived three days after the funeral. I was deprived of seeing her in life and also when she died. I was terribly hurt, and I still am.

Although my Uncle Oscar, Aunt Molly, and father had cemetery plots on Long Island, my mother was buried somewhere in New Jersey. My father's friend was a member of a Jewish men's lodge that owned grave sites out there, and Mr. Mestel, Poppa's friend, could get him a plot. Even in death she was separated from the family.

Several years ago I made up my mind to find her grave. The problem was that no one knew where she was buried. I called my three sisters. None of them could remember where she was interred, or sadly enough, even the day she died. They had blocked it out.

My mother was a missing person. The only clue we had to the location of her burial site was a receipt from the company that had carved her headstone. I called the owner, Al Abramawitz. He said he had bought the business very recently from another company but still had the previous owner's records, though they were not computerized.

Mr. Abramawitz called back an hour later with the news that he had found the record of my mother's burial. Helen died on April 15, 1958, and was buried at Mount Moriah Cemetery in Fairview, New Jersey. My sisters thought she had been buried in 1968. They were off by ten years. They were still in denial about her death.

On a beautiful Sunday morning in March 2003, my sister Alice, my son, Joel, and I drove out to Mount Moriah. We had the location of the grave.

I didn't know what to expect. Alice had known our mother because she was six years older. I hadn't known her at all.

As we walked along the rows of gravestones, I kept reading names. I didn't know any of them, but they reminded me of my own mortality. Mother's gravestone was in the last row. It was dark gray. The carved letters read:

Helen Buchwald
Died April 15, 1958
Beloved Wife and
Devoted Mother

Alice and I stared in silence for several minutes. I felt I was at the end of a long journey and the circle had now been closed.

Standing at graveside, Alice began talking about Mother. She said she was beautiful, Orthodox, and a very tough cookie. Alice remembered Mother's rule that before she could eat even a slice of bread she had to say a prayer.

Edith and Alice had visited her in the state hospital over the years. Sometimes Mother knew who they were and sometimes she thought they were girls who worked for Pop. Here is a funny thing about visiting the cemetery: Mother's gravestone was a foot taller than all the others around her.

As we left Mount Moriah, Alice and I laughed.

Pop

Though I never had the chance with my mother, I did attend my father's funeral.

All my life I had a strange relationship with Father. He was a Sunday father. Since my sisters and I were living in foster homes, he came on Sundays to visit. By the time I was sixteen, I saw him on a daily basis, but we didn't have much to say to each other. We slept in the kitchen together (the girls had the bedroom). He was really a good man, and a kind man. But he had no control over me.

He used to say, "You dasn't do this," and

"You dasn't do that." I didn't argue, I just did as I pleased. I was his only son and I hurt him — first when I refused to be bar mitzvahed, then when I ran away from home and joined the Marines, and finally when I moved to Paris. He couldn't understand why I wanted to become a writer. When it turned out I made a living at it, Dad couldn't tell me how proud he was. But later my sisters told me he carried my articles in his pocket and showed them to everybody.

My father worked very hard sewing and hanging curtains and draperies, but he never made much money at it. The joke in the family was that if he had been successful, I would now be the president of the Aetna Curtain Company.

Joseph Buchwald was five feet eight inches tall, and very strong because he carried the drapes and curtains on the subway. He worked until the day before he died at age seventy-nine. I remember seeing him a week before he passed away; he was talking about dying, and I said, "You dasn't do that." He smiled.

When he did die, on July 6, 1972, the funeral services were held in a temple in Forest Hills. Fifteen minutes before the service the rabbi called me into his office and said, "So tell me something about your father." I was not in a good mood. "Rabbi," I said, "you never knew my father and you can't do a canned eulogy about him."

"What can I say?" the rabbi asked.

"Say the prayers and that's enough."

My father was buried on Long Island and I cried because we never got to know each other. I mourned him, mainly for the lonely life he led after my mother was put away, living in one room in the Bronx. I still talk to him and I tell him, "I am sorry that I wasn't bar mitzvahed, Pop."

9
FINAL
ARRANGEMENTS

A Good Surrogate

The two important pieces of business you have to attend to before you climb the golden stairs are a regular will and a living will.

The regular will spells out to whom you want to leave your worldly goods. If there are a lot of worldly goods, it's better to have it done with a lawyer.

Disinheriting someone can be almost as much fun as inheriting them. Attitudes toward loved ones change all the time.

It's the last power trip you can take.

Some people leave money they don't have to a church or charity. In my case, my wife pretended she had half a million dollars to leave to the bishop. She didn't have it. Since I don't go to confession, I wasn't bothered by cutting him off.

One of the games people play has to do with which heirs you want to leave money to and which ones you want to leave out. The last year of your life is very important when it comes to writing a will. There are several people I had mentioned in my will, but when I got mad at them I crossed them out.

If you want to be kept in somebody's will, be nice and give him a box of candy.

The living will has to do with making all your wishes known before you die. You must tell someone if you want to be kept on life support (or not), how you want to get buried, what kind of funeral you want, and how much you want spent on a coffin.

One day I read a story in *The Washington Post* about appointing a surrogate to make decisions for you if you should become incapacitated by illness.

My question is, whom can you trust to make such serious decisions?

I've always been under the impression that a surrogate would do exactly what an ill person requests. But this is not necessarily true. Rick Weiss, who wrote the *Post* article, pointed out that according to a survey by the National Institutes of Health, surrogates often do not fulfill the wishes of the patient. The survey participants, who were volunteer patients, were asked to imagine that they were incapacitated. Their designated surrogates, who were given descriptions of the patients' medical circumstances, were supposed to make a decision about what the loved one really wanted. The surrogates got it right only 68 percent of the time.

In the study, doctors didn't have any better idea about when the patients wanted the plug pulled. In fact they fared worse — making the correct choice only 63 percent of the time.

And here you are thinking that if anything happens to you, your surrogate will do exactly what you want.

I will give you an example. The son in this story was the surrogate, and he said he knew precisely what his father would want if he were to become incapacitated. He wanted the plug to be pulled. The daughter insisted the father wanted to hang around for a much longer time. The problem here is that one family member may claim to know what the patient wants, but another will claim he wants just the opposite.

This opens a whole can of worms about families, because in times of crisis everybody has their own opinion as to what their loved one wants. The son says, "Dad would want to go right now, peacefully," and the daughter says, "He told me he wanted to hang in there as long as he could," and then a third family member says, "Neither one of you knows what Dad wanted because I was the only one who ever saw him."

You can see the difficulty we're in. The kicker is that in the study, it turns out that 70 percent of patients changed their minds.

It's a very tough thing to figure out, and all I can say is pick a surrogate (family member, lawyer, whatever) before you become incapacitated — then make sure that person knows exactly what you want.

I think of myself because people are naturally selfish. I want a surrogate who is certain to know what I want when it's time to say goodbye.

I'm not being grim about this. Besides everything I have mentioned, things could become even dicier when money is involved. Then the question is, are we worried about the wishes of the patient or about the money involved?

These are the decisions that we all face. For every person who is incapacitated there has to be a surrogate standing by — and a good surrogate is hard to find.

My Plan

The important thing about a hospice is if you can stay long enough you can say good-bye with dignity, and also plan your own funeral. It gives you something to do after you finish reading *Vanity Fair.*

My plan was quite simple. Joseph Gawler's Sons Funeral Home was down the street from my hospice, so I didn't have far to go. I chose cremation for no other reason than it would be easier to transport me to my cemetery plot on Martha's Vineyard, where Ann is buried.

I'll stay at Gawler's for one night. Then Joel, my son, will keep my ashes at his house in Washington until they can be taken to Martha's Vineyard, either by plane or by car — whichever is cheaper.

As I'm planning my funeral, I keep adding details all the time.

I make sure my obituary appears in *The New York Times.* As I've mentioned, no one knows whether you've lived or died unless they read it in the *Times.* I also make sure no head of state or Nobel Prize winner dies on the same day. I don't want them to use up my space.

I insist that my obituary not say, "He died after a long illness." I want it to read, "He died at the age of 98 on a private tennis court, just after he aced Andre Agassi."

My funeral is a small private affair on Martha's Vineyard. The navy's Blue Angels will fly over, members of the Vineyard

Haven Yacht Club will drop their sails, and golfers will observe a minute of silence.

Friends on the island will gather at my grave site and sing "Danny Boy" — my favorite song, though I am Jewish.

After the service everyone will go back to the Styrons' for cocktails. I keep my funeral simple, because, as Walter Cronkite says, "Arthur wanted it that way."

A note on my cemetery plot: Peter Feibleman, a friend and writer, and I were taking a walk on Martha's Vineyard along the road to West Chop one summer day in the mid 1980s when we passed a family cemetery. It belonged to the Look family, and upon closer inspection we found out that the first Look to be buried there was Thomas Look, in 1743.

A man inside the cemetery was digging a hole with a shovel.

Peter asked him, "How's business?"

The man said, "It's getting better. We're adding twenty-five sites which the county intends to sell."

"How come?" I asked.

"There are no living members of the Look family left to pay maintenance."

"Can anyone purchase a plot?"

"If you have five hundred dollars and

don't buy it for a profit."

Peter and I looked at each other, then rushed back to tell the gang.

Bill and Rose Styron said, "We'll take two." Mary and Mike Wallace said, "Put us down for a pair." John and Barbara Hersey said they were in. Lucy and Sheldon Hackney (Sheldon was then the president of the University of Pennsylvania) and Ann and I said we each wanted two. My friend Peter, who wasn't married, took two on "spec." He said he wanted to sleep next to the woman he loved for eternity.

A week later, after doing the county paperwork, we all went down to the cemetery to pick out our plots. People behave strangely in a cemetery. Rose Styron said, "I want to be over there." Then she changed her mind and said, "I want to be over here. No, I've changed my mind — over there."

Bill said, "Wallpaper — she is picking out wallpaper."

Mike and Mary Wallace said they didn't want to be near the road as it was too noisy.

I told Ann, "Let's pick a plot under the oak tree so we don't have to be buried with suntan oil."

When our friend Jules Feiffer, the cartoonist, heard about the plan, he called us the "Nouveau Dead."

Peter Feibleman picked two spots near the gate. As luck would have it, that summer he met the girl of his dreams. He fell in love with Carol Burnett, the TV and motion picture star. And she fell in love with him.

Like any man in love, Peter gave Carol one of his plots.

Sadly, when the summer was over, Carol was no longer in love, and she wrote me a letter in which she said, "I no longer want to be buried on Martha's Vineyard with Peter. I want to be buried on Maui, next to Lindbergh."

I replied, "A deal is a deal, but the gang is offering a very reasonable compromise. If you get cremated you can spend six months in Maui and six months on Martha's Vineyard."

Selecting the Urn

Early in my hospice stay I kept pestering Joel about going over to Joseph Gawler's Sons Funeral Home on Wisconsin Avenue to select an urn for the cremation. I think he was stalling, but finally I pressed him into it.

We had to get an ambulance for me to get over there. I have been to Gawler's many times, so I was familiar with its rooms. The funeral director showed us to the room that had all the urns in it. The least expensive ones were around $500, but I was told we could go up to $4,000.

Here is a partial estimate that Gawler's gave us for a first-class cremation in early 2006:

- Direct cremation with container — $4,300
- Cremation container — $1,600 to $2,800
- Cremation-oriented casket — $3,500 to $16,000
- Crematory fee — $350
- Online Internet Memorial/Archive — $295
- Use of Facilities and Staff Services for Visitation, including coordinating the funeral arrangements, supervision of funeral, and staff to assist with the funeral ceremony — $800 per day
- Equipment and Staff Services for Service at the Crematory, including accompaniment of remains to crematory, supervision of service, display of floral arrangements, and staff to assist at the service — $900
- Use of Reception/Hospitality Room and supervision during reception — $800

- Urns — $900 to $11,000
- Flowers — $25 to $10,000
- Clothing — $100 to $5,000

The funeral director estimated that what we wanted would cost about $10,000. We thanked him and told him he would see us again.

I later asked Joel to describe his feelings at that time. This is what he wrote:

Dad kept asking me to take him to a funeral home. He really wanted to plan all his details. His bugging me about it went on for a week. My main concerns were transportation and logistics. Several weeks earlier, I had arranged for Dad to visit the Washington Hospice. I'd gotten a wheelchair van. Dad was wheeled into it and then strapped down — a twenty-minute process — and then the van proceeded to break down three times on the fifteen-minute ride to the Washington Hospice. Dad was stuck in the wheelchair and despondent. We eventually made it, but the whole event was traumatic for both of us.

When Dad wanted to visit the funeral home I kept picturing our past transport disaster, and tried to avoid the trip for as long as possible.

He pushed until I gave in, so we hired Mo, a friend of Dad's who is also a taxi driver and has his own station wagon. Getting Dad in and out of the car wasn't as hard as I thought it would be. We even stopped at McDonald's on the way home to celebrate. (No breakdowns.)

The actual visit to the funeral home wasn't too bad; a little surreal, but given the past few months, this was like adding another car to the circus train heading down the tracks of life.

I had contacted the funeral home previously and a funeral director was waiting for us. He gave us a tour of the facility, but we were already familiar with it because in 1994, when Mom died, we had her visitation there.

Dad was curious about the urns, so the director took us through their display room, which was filled with all sorts of urns at various prices. Dad settled on the inexpensive white one.

They also had keepsake urns in which a few of the ashes would be placed. I picked out a couple of urns, in case some relatives would want one. My nephew Ben wanted one to take to Paris, where he would toss the ashes off the Eiffel Tower.

My sister Connie, who worked part time at a funeral home in Culpeper, Virginia, delivering corpses, would pick out her own keepsake urn at her funeral home. My other sister, Jennifer, heard that we had been to the funeral home and eventually wanted all the information, so I gave her a card from the director.

Dad wanted to feed and water all the people who might come to pay their respects. The director offered to provide catering and Dad settled on finger food.

He also was curious about the room where the visitation would take place and the placement of the urn. The funeral home had a contraption that looked like it was right out of *Raiders of the Lost Ark*. The urn would be placed in the ark to be carried wherever it needed to go.

After spending a morning at the funeral home, the McDonald's ice cream tasted especially good.

The Memorial Service

Wait — there is a lot more. I haven't told you about my memorial service in New York, to be held a week after my burial on Martha's Vineyard. The service takes place at Carnegie Hall.

After I am cremated, my ashes are col-

70

lected and, during the memorial celebration, they are sprinkled over every Trump building in New York City.

The rules for my memorial are that everyone must leave his or her watch at the door so they won't be checking the time during the service.

Kleenex is provided.

I weighed carefully whether there should be a day off for schoolchildren, but decided against it when the mayor said it would cost the city overtime and snarl up the traffic.

As they enter, the mourners will be given a handout that says, "In lieu of flowers, the family requests that you make contributions to the Brady anti-gun lobby" — my favorite charity.

The Harlem Boys Choir will sing "Going Home," the New York Symphony will play "I Love Paris," and Pavarotti will sing "The Marines' Hymn."

The New York City Police bagpipe band will play in the street before the service starts. Flags will be flown at half-mast on every hospital that treats depression and a moment of silence will be observed.

I have been very careful about choosing the people I want to speak at the memorial. Too many times, a speaker will talk more about himself than the dearly departed. I recall one eulogy that went like this: "We are here to say goodbye to Davey. I had lunch with him a week before he died. I remember it well because I had Dover sole with a lobster sauce and a bottle of Montrachet 1999."

The rabbi at my service will share a few words to warm up the crowd. I don't know him, so whatever he says has to be taken with a grain of salt. Cardinal Egan also speaks and reads a letter from the pope. Billy Graham will read one from the president. I figure that among the three of them, I'm covering all the bases; one of them is bound to have some idea where I am going.

I don't want any politicians to speak, because my mourners would think I'd sold out.

The way I see it, Carnegie Hall is jammed, and thousands of people are standing on Fifty-seventh Street, even though it is snowing. The memorial service is the hottest ticket in New York. Scalpers are selling orchestra seats for $250.

After saying kind things about me, Mike Wallace and Bill Styron talk about my depression and what it meant to them. People in the street listen to every word and watch on a large TV screen. The service is televised on NBC, ABC, CBS, CNN, the

BBC, and Court TV.

No detail is too small to consider.

The thing I am proudest of is that I provide parking in Central Park for all the chauffeured limousines. I assume my friends will arrive in style. This does not mean the people driving their own cars will be ignored. We will have valet parking for them on Columbus Circle.

If I must say so myself, it will be one of the most celebrated memorial services New York has ever seen.

People will talk about it for years.

10
THE SALON

The beauty of not dying, but expecting to, is that it gives you a chance to say goodbye to everybody. When I thought I'd only be here for two weeks, I figured it wasn't enough time to bid my goodbyes, but now, because I've been here so long, I've been able to say farewell to relatives, friends, and strangers. Some of them have such a good time they come back again and again.

So far, I've heard from everybody in my life — from my public school days, the University of Southern California, the Marine Corps, my Paris pals, and all the people I knew or who claimed they knew me in Washington. I received nearly three thousand letters, many of them from people who were connected to me (or thought they were) in some way. I had met them in Paris, or I'd spoken at their graduation. Then the visitors started to arrive. Every letter, phone call, and visit made me remember an incident or a little gift from the past.

From the Halls of Montezuma . . .

The commandant of the United States Marine Corps, General Mike Hagee, visited me and I told him all about my life in the Marines, which was quite different from his. Like all Marines, I inflated the role I played during World War II.

When Tom Brokaw called wanting to know why the commandant had come to see me, I said, "They just found out I put the flag on Iwo Jima."

I told General Hagee that I was in a fighter squadron and I cleaned guns. Whether he was impressed, I'm not sure. You never question another Marine's credibility. I told him that at the end of the war I talked myself into being a publicity man for the Cherry Point, North Carolina, Marine Corps football team. The team wasn't very good, but since the war was over, my only job was to make them sound fantastic. We played a big game in Washington against the Air Transport Command. We lost, 37 to nothing.

All the top brass who had read my glowing press releases had bet on Cherry Point. It was after that game that they called me in and suggested I might want to leave the Corps.

Many years later, in 1999, General Jim Jones (who was the commandant at that time) gave me a parade on Eighth and I streets at the Marine Corps barracks. If you haven't been in the Marine Corps, you might not know this was a super honor. I think I got it for my column, and not for my service in the war.

Among all my hospice visits, the one from the commandant was the most exciting. As soon as he left, I called everyone I had served with and told them to eat their hearts out.

Dying Wish

It is amazing how many people visit if you are in a convenient location and they've been told you're going to die. I take full advantage of my situation in order to get people to do things for me.

For example, the dean of a fancy California university who is also a good friend called and asked if I wanted anything or if he could bring anything. I replied, "Yes, my dying wish is this: Would you arrange for two young friends of mine to get into the freshman class?" It was a weird request, and I doubt the dean has ever been asked to fulfill a dying wish of that kind, but he said,

"If it's really your dying wish, I'll try."

By chance (or not), both girls got in. I made not only the two girls happy, but also their parents and grandparents. The grandfather of one of the girls sent me three cheesecakes and three food baskets from Zabar's.

From Childhood Past

I saw my life passing through my hospice living room. Twenty alumni from the Hebrew Orphan Asylum showed up to visit. I was briefly a ward of the HOA in 1930. When I was five years old my father had moved my sisters and me from the home in Flushing with the Seventh Day Adventist nurses to the Hebrew Orphan Asylum on Amsterdam Avenue in New York City. I was there only two months in quarantine before being placed in my first foster home, but I made friendships that last to this day.

All of the HOA visitors to the hospice were in their eighties, and their leader was Norman Rales, a very successful industrialist. They sang songs to me that we had learned at the institution.

Other alumni of the orphanage found out about my being in the Washington Hospice and put a notice in their newsletter asking everyone to call and write to me. The funny thing was, they all claimed to be my bunk-mate. What they didn't know was that I never spent time in a bunk in the orphanage.

I heard from kids I knew in Public School 35 in Hollis, New York. Some of the remaining members of the Happy Girls Club wrote to me. They were an informal sorority who did everything together in public school. I used to hang around with them on my roller skates. I was their mascot. Even in elementary school they flirted. Years later the girls bought tickets for the second balcony to see my play, *Sheep on the Runway*. They called themselves "Artie's groupies."

I heard from pals in the Marine Corps, some who hadn't considered me a pal when I was in their outfit. Back then, when they weren't nice to me I blamed them for not liking Jewish Marines. One tentmate of mine said at the time, "They don't dislike you because you are Jewish, but because you are an asshole."

People who had been in my life sent me souvenirs from the times we had been together. They sent me photographs, newspaper clippings, and articles about Eniwetok in the Marshall Islands.

My USC college buddies sent me clippings of my stories in the *Daily Trojan* newspaper and *Wampus* magazine.

Me and Picasso

After my media splash, some letter writers relayed memories of eating in a Paris restaurant with me. I had taken them around Les Halles. They remembered sitting with me at Fouquet's sidewalk café.

One of the most interesting columns I'd written in Paris was one about how silly my mail was getting. To illustrate my point I printed a letter from Harvey Brodsky, a student at Temple University in Philadelphia.

Harvey said he was in love with a girl named Gloria Segall, and he hoped to marry her someday. She claimed to be the greatest living fan of Pablo Picasso.

The couple went to a Picasso exhibit, and to impress her, Harvey told Gloria that he could probably get Picasso's autograph. Harvey's letter continued, "Since that incident Gloria and I have stopped seeing each other. I did a stupid thing and she told me she never wanted to see me again. I'm writing to you because I'm not giving up on Gloria. Could you get Picasso's autograph for me? If you could, I have a feeling Gloria and I could get back together. The futures of two young people depend on it. I know she is miserable without me and I without her. Everything depends on you." At the end of the letter he said, "I, Harvey Brodsky, do solemnly swear that any item received by me from Art Buchwald (namely, Pablo Picasso's autograph) will never be sold or given to anyone except Miss Gloria Segall."

I printed the letter in my column to show how ridiculous my mail was. When it appeared, David Duncan, an American photographer, was with Picasso in Cannes and Duncan translated it for Picasso. Picasso was very moved, and he took out his crayons and drew a beautiful color sketch for Gloria and signed it, "Pour Gloria."

Duncan called and told me the good news.

I said, "The heck with Gloria Segall, what about me?"

Duncan explained this to Picasso, and in crayons he drew a picture of the two of us together, holding glasses of wine, and wrote on the top, "Pour Art Buchwald."

By this time the Associated Press had picked up the story, and they followed through on the delivery of the picture to Gloria Segall. When it arrived via special delivery in Philadelphia, Gloria took one look and said, "Harvey and I will always be good friends."

If you're wondering how the story ends,

Harvey married somebody else, and so did Gloria. The Picasso hangs in Gloria's living room.

It was a story that caught the imagination of people all over the world. I received a flood of letters after the column was published. My favorite came from an art dealer in New York. "I can find you as many unhappy couples in New York City as you can get Picasso sketches. One girl said she is on the verge of suicide if she doesn't hear from Picasso, and I know several couples in Greenwich Village who are in the initial stages of divorce. Please wire me how many autographs you can get. We both stand to make a fortune."

Another letter, from Johnny Kohn in London, said, "My wife threatens to leave me unless I can get her Khrushchev's autograph. She would like it signed on a Russian sable coat."

The final chapter of this story takes place in the hospice, where Harvey Brodsky and Gloria showed up for a visit. They hadn't married each other, but they both maintained that the Gloria Segall Picasso changed their lives.

I know my Picasso has to be worth a lot of money, but my children won't let me sell it.

Holding Grudges

Another visitor was Pierce O'Donnell, my lawyer during my lawsuit in the 1980s against Paramount Pictures. Back then, I claimed they had stolen my idea for the film *Coming to America*. Pierce took the case on contingency, and it lasted eight years. Since the film had to do with Eddie Murphy, I became famous — something I obviously have been trying to do all my life.

I was never a screenwriter, but one day in 1977 I had an idea for a movie. I was sitting in the Rose Garden of the White House, where President Carter was entertaining the Shah of Iran. Outside the gates, thousands of Iranian students with paper bags on their heads protested the Shah's visit to the United States. The students made such an uproar that the police fired tear gas at them. The tear gas blew into the Rose Garden and both President Carter and the Shah started to cry.

I watched the scene, and the premise for a movie hit me. Suppose a ruling prince came to Washington, D.C., on a state visit and was overthrown back home by his brother-in-law with the help of the CIA.

All the prince's bank accounts are frozen, he is tossed out of the White House, and he winds up in the ghetto, where he sees life as it really is.

I wrote a treatment and sent it to my friend Alain Bernheim, who was a Hollywood producer. Alain sent it to Paramount as an idea for Eddie Murphy. The studio took an option for a year and the contract read that if they made the movie, Alain and I would get 25 percent of the net profits.

Just before the option ran out, Paramount said it was not interested in the project and returned it to us, saying it wasn't right for Eddie Murphy. Then we brought the treatment to Twentieth Century-Fox. While they were reading it, Paramount announced it was making a movie about an African prince who comes to America, starring Eddie Murphy.

Obviously, Twentieth was no longer interested in our project. When *Coming to America* was finally released, I saw it on Martha's Vineyard. When it was over, I called my partner Alain and said, "Let's sue."

The major studios had been screwing people for years and someone had to have the guts to take them on. When the lawsuit was announced it became a daily front-page story. Eddie was a superstar and Paramount was not going to allow bad press to disturb him. Besides, Eddie Murphy put his name on the picture as the sole writer of the story.

Marty Davis, then the president of Paramount Pictures, whom I knew, took our suit personally. Marty was known as the King of Chutzpah. While the suit was on, one of his aides called me and said, "Marty is being honored at the Waldorf next month as a great writer and he wants you to be the speaker."

I said, "For Christ's sakes, doesn't he know I'm suing him?"

The aide said, "Marty says one thing has nothing to do with the other."

As the suit progressed, the press wrote that I was David and Paramount was Goliath. I rather saw myself as Rocky. Every time I walked down Rodeo Drive I expected music to come up and the screenwriters to cheer.

That was the good part.

What I didn't know at the time is the lengths to which lawyers will go to win a case. They will try to destroy you as a writer and a person. They will dig up personal facts to make you look like a serial killer.

Once the judge in my case decided that I wrote the original idea, Paramount said I stole it from Charlie Chaplin's *King of New York*. The accusation went around the world on the wire services. When Judge Schneider ruled the next day that I hadn't stolen the idea, the truth hardly received a mention.

The case went on for eight years. We won in court after four years of trial and then Judge Schneider ruled we were entitled to net, and then the penalty phase stretched on for four more.

We assumed our net was at least ten million dollars, but Paramount maintained that although *Coming to America* at that point had made $250 million ($600 million to this day), the picture had lost money. *There was no net.*

The studio had written off every turkey they made that year as well as rent, heat, hot water, bonuses for executives, and private planes. As Larry Gelbart, the creator of the *M*A*S*H* TV series, told me, "There is no net when you are entitled to net."

The judge said we had to get something.

Paramount said it would appeal. Four years later, Frank Biondi, then head of Paramount, decided to settle rather than appeal. Alain and I received $900,000 to divide between us.

Everyone at Paramount told us the suit was business, but to this day I consider it personal. Everyone who has to deal with lawyers takes it personally. By this time I hope you know how I feel about lawyers. I still dream up different ways to kill them. Because I lived in France, the death that gives me the most pleasure is seeing the entire Paramount legal team waiting their turn to be guillotined.

As I've mentioned, the beauty of the hospice and all the attention I have received from the press and television is that everyone knows where to find me. I received one call from a gentleman who said his name was Harvey and he was calling to wish me well and hoped I was not in pain.

I thanked him and then said, "Who are you?"

He said, "Harvey Schneider. I was the judge in your *Coming to America* suit against Paramount."

And I said, "Oh, I'm so glad to hear from you. Is there any more money there?"

He laughed and said, "I'll reread the transcript."

The Academy

Russell Baker, the *New York Times* columnist emeritus, also came to visit, and we had much to share. His column in the *Times* was funny, witty, and erudite. All the things I hated him for. We used to meet for lunch to discuss how bad the world was. Baker was far more downbeat than I. He felt the world would end tomorrow. I gave it about three days.

One day we were eating lunch at the Sans Souci, a power restaurant near the White House. (Now a McDonald's.)

Baker and I lunched there several times a week, but one day when he paid the check he complained that we had no reason to continue having lunch. All we were doing was hoping to steal column ideas from each other. "Besides, you are not much fun to eat with," he said.

"And neither are you," I retorted. "We have to find a new reason to lunch. What if we founded a luncheon club like they have at Princeton?"

Baker said, "It doesn't have enough prestige. Why not an academy?"

"How about the Academy of Humor Columnists?"

Baker countered, "The American Academy of Humor Columnists. We don't want anyone to think we are communists."

"We should have swords like the French Academy, and a secret handshake."

"The first order of business is the initiation fee."

"Who should we ask to join?" I asked.

"Calvin Trillin?"

"Art Hoppe of the *San Francisco*

Chronicle. He has always wanted to break into the East Coast Establishment."

We decided we needed a token African American. "What about Don Ross, who writes a humor column for that Oklahoma paper? If he can't afford to pay the dues we'll get him a grant from the Ford Foundation."

"Do we have to have a woman?"

"Why not Erma Bombeck?" I suggested. "She is very funny and makes three times as much money as we do."

We kept adding candidates: Jerry Nachman of the *Daily News,* Andy Rooney, Garry Trudeau, and Dave Barry, who was a snotty kid since he kept stealing newspaper clients from us.

It was a very productive lunch, and as soon as we got back to our respective offices we sent out letters to those on our list announcing they were elected and asking them to make out their tax-deductible initiation checks to the Academy.

To make sure they opened the letters, we printed on the envelope "You Have Just Won Five Million Dollars" — an idea we stole from the *Reader's Digest.*

The columnists wrote back they were flattered to be nominated to the Academy, and of course the check was in the mail.

Responses followed from Baker and me in letters to members. We wrote Erma she had to sweep the clubhouse floor and make sure the spittoons were polished every morning.

We wrote Don Ross and told him he wasn't very funny and he had to stick to his "Roots."

Baker dispatched a letter to Andy Rooney telling him he had been made a member of the Academy, but since he had reached the mandatory retirement age of sixty-five he had to resign.

For two years the letters went back and forth, each member putting more effort into the correspondence than they put into their columns.

One of the more famous exchanges had to do with a fruitcake. Russ Baker sent me a fruitcake he had received for Christmas. He said he had lost three teeth trying to bite into it. He wanted me to have it as a token of our friendship.

I didn't know what to do with it, but I remembered that Erma Bombeck was building a new house and decided the fruitcake would be perfect as a brick for the fireplace. I sent it to her. Instead of accepting it, Erma mailed it back to Russ with a Black & Decker drill so he could get the raisins out of his teeth.

Erma is no longer with us. Russ is retired and does volunteer work on *Masterpiece Theater.* Don Ross went into Oklahoma politics, and Dave Barry turns out a book every other week.

Calvin Trillin works for *The New Yorker,* the only magazine that will have him. Andy Rooney is still on *60 Minutes* telling us why he hates milk cartons.

Garry Trudeau is still irreverent about the administration, which makes him a traitor or a left-wing liberal or both.

The Academy no longer exists. It went bankrupt after Russ and I started cooking the books.

Since it really didn't exist except in our minds, a funny thing happened when we went to the mailbox. Robert Yoakum, who had a column servicing two or three papers, demanded we make him a member. He was serious and kept sending us letters and having friends intervene for him. It got so bad Baker said, "Let's make Yoakum the main reason for the Academy — to keep Yoakum out."

The Gang

The usual suspects who come to visit me are George Stevens, Jr., Jack Valenti, Ben Bradlee, and Joe Califano, otherwise known as "the gang." The girlfriends include Ethel Kennedy, Bonnie Nelson Schwartz, Kathy Kemper, Sue Bailey, Diane Machan, and Linda Mortenson. Since I have only one leg I can flirt with them and they aren't afraid to flirt back. It is a wonderful game.

Jack Valenti has stopped by many times. I first met Jack when he was President Johnson's special assistant in the White House. We got to be pals in 1964 when he asked me to work on Johnson's first Gridiron speech. Jack, Bill Moyers, and I worked on it as a comedy team and we leaned on some writers from Hollywood. It took us two or three weeks to get the speech in shape. The night of the dinner, Johnson listened to several skits about himself. He didn't laugh much. The writing team and I were all waiting for him to go on to deliver the speech we had crafted. Finally he got up and he said, "Thank you for this wonderful dinner." And he sat down. We couldn't believe it. Two weeks later I was at a reception at Abe Fortas's house and Abe introduced me to the president. Johnson grabbed my hand in both of his and said, "Art, I'll never be able to thank you enough for the wonderful job you did on my Gridiron speech."

Jack went on to be the head of the Motion Picture Association of America, where he claimed he never saw a film he didn't like.

Another of my frequent visitors, George Stevens, Jr., produces the Kennedy Center Honors programs. He booked me to be the first stand-up commentator for the show in 1978. My monologue, addressed to Jimmy Carter, had to do with how the Kennedy Center was built:

Mr. President, since you have only lived in Washington for a couple of years, I am sure you cannot fully appreciate what it means for the rest of us to devote an entire evening in this town to culture.

To understand the importance of this evening, Mr. President, you have to imagine what the cultural scene was like in Washington before there was a Kennedy Center. On this very site, only a few years ago, there were buffalo as far as the eye could see. Up on Capitol Hill there were nothing but saloons filled with hard-drinking politicians and free-spending South Koreans. There was no place a respectable person could take his family for a cup of coffee or a glass of Amaretto.

But into this vast cultural wasteland came a man named Roger Stevens, who had made a personal fortune in real estate, selling the Brooklyn Bridge to the Chase Manhattan Bank. One night Roger had a dream. He dreamt he could build a cultural center on the banks of the Potomac River for forty million dollars — but he overslept. And by the time he woke up it was seventy million dollars. So Roger went to the Senate Armed Services Committee, whose powerful chairman told him, "Boy, if you want a cultural center for Washington, D.C., you're going to have to build it in Mississippi."

Roger was about to give up on his idea when a lobbyist told him, "You're not going to get any money by telling Congress you want to build a cultural center. If you say you want to build a missile site they'll buy it in a minute."

"You mean with these architectural plans?" Roger said.

"Sure. Your blueprints call for a roof that opens at the top, and that's exactly what a missile site needs."

So Roger went back to the Senate and said, "I changed my mind. Instead of a cultural center, I want to build a missile site to protect the Watergate from a sneak attack."

"Now you're *talking,* boy," the chairman

said. "How much do you need?"

"Twenty million dollars," Roger said.

"Take sixty, and keep the change."

Mr. President, be grateful for small favors. If it weren't for men like Roger Stevens, you would now be sitting in Lafayette Park on a cold, wet wooden bench listening to a high school band playing "Hail to the Redskins." It may not be my place to say, sir, but culturally speaking, you came to the right place at the right time.

When I was doing well in the hospice, George accused me of pulling a scam, and said I was just in it for the money.

Ben Bradlee, who was editor of *The Washington Post,* comes to see me every day. He was my friend in Paris and in Washington. I considered him my equal until Watergate, when he became more famous than Jason Robards. I have only two complaints about Ben: He never told me who "Deep Throat" was, and in forty years he never gave me a raise for writing my column.

Ben was one of John F. Kennedy's closest friends. The day Kennedy was killed I was returning from Charleston, West Virginia, after making a speech. As I got out of a taxi at the National Press Building I saw people running in and out of the building.

"What's up?" I asked.

"Kennedy's been shot."

I flew upstairs to the *Newsweek* Washington bureau where Ben was. He was in shock. We both watched the TV hoping against hope that Kennedy was still alive.

Finally, Walter Cronkite announced he was dead. Ben and I hugged each other and we cried.

Joe Califano, another close friend, comes to see me in the hospice. Years ago, when Joe was made Secretary of Health, Education, and Welfare under President Jimmy Carter, he invited me to go to China with a delegation of doctors, educators, and press.

When we arrived in Beijing, Joe was standing at the bottom of the stairs to the plane, introducing everyone in his party to the Chinese Minister of Health.

When he got to me he said, "This is Mr. Buchwald. He is a humorist."

This was translated and Joe asked, "Do you know what a humorist is?"

The minister nodded his head.

The next morning when I came down for breakfast I said "Good morning" to the members of the Chinese delegation and they started laughing. For the next nine days, no matter what I said, my hosts laughed.

On the last night, Califano held a banquet in Beijing. He asked me to speak for the press.

After seven Gambays (cognacs) I stood up and said,

I wish to thank all the people who made our trip so wonderful. The People's Republic knows how to treat the press. In America we would never be invited to sit in a banquet like this. We would be out in the rain waiting for news of any kind.

I want to thank the people who went through my luggage in my hotel room while we were at dinner to make sure my socks and shirts were in the right place. And the people who listened in on my telephone calls to my wife to make sure I had a clear line.

But mostly I would like to thank the man who went from city to city with us and had the top of his head removed to prove acupuncture works.

After one more Gambay I passed out.

Joe Califano used to drive me to the Redskin games. I don't know if this will get me in hot water or not, but he was the worst driver I have ever been with. He thought he was in a NASCAR race and never stopped for red lights.

Name-Dropping in the Hospice

Former astronaut and senator John Glenn has come to see me three times so far. He isn't a stranger. Our first connection came when I wrote about him and six other astronauts in my column in 1962. We became more closely acquainted when he was elected to the Senate. He was a Democratic speaker at the Gridiron Club dinner and asked me to help him be funny. I worked on his speech with several other people. I loved him, but we had trouble getting him to tell a joke. As we put him through his paces he kept asking, "When can I be serious?" And we kept saying, "Wait, John, wait."

Since I'm name-dropping, the Queen of Swaziland came to the hospice with an entourage of ten beautiful women and ten courtiers. The queen was inspecting hospices for her country. She was gorgeous, dressed in Paris couturier clothes, as were her attendants. Chris Turner, the hospice clinical services manager, asked me in front of the queen, "Art, how do you like this place?" "It's terrible," I replied. "They beat you and starve you. It's just like Abu Ghraib." Fortunately, the queen had a sense of humor and everybody laughed.

Another visitor was Donald Rumsfeld. I knew Rumsfeld when he was Jerry Ford's chief of staff. He was a good guy and we played tennis together with Ethel Kennedy and Secretary of the Treasury Bill Simon. I recall that one of the times we played, a Secret Service agent came out on the court and said to Rumsfeld, "There's a call for you," and Rummy replied, "Well, tell the president I'll call him back." The Secret Service agent said in a nervous voice, "It isn't the president, it's Henry Kissinger."

I must admit I haven't been kind to Rumsfeld lately because we are of different political persuasions. I didn't discuss Iraq with him during the visit. Instead, I told him if he was going to resign or get fired, I could get him a room here at the hospice.

One visitor who keeps coming back all the time is Ambassador Joe Wilson. He was the one who went to Niger for the CIA to find out if they were selling uranium to Iraq. Wilson's wife, Valerie Plame, was a CIA agent.

Ms. Plame was supposed to be protected from willful disclosure of the identity of a Central Intelligence Agency officer. In his column, Robert Novak identified her and indicated she was the one who sent Wilson to Niger. A special prosecutor was on the case for several years investigating the leak.

I knew Wilson from Martha's Vineyard, and on his own he came to the hospice to visit me. He came several times. The joke was that because his wife was writing a book, she wanted him to stay out of the house. I asked him why he didn't write another book and he said, "This is my year to play golf."

We talked about Africa, on which Wilson is very well informed, and we had our own think tank at the hospice.

The White House was furious with Wilson and it was fun to have an inside look at "Bush's War."

My hospice living room was a place he loved to visit.

Valerie also visited. It isn't important, but she is very beautiful and the three of us had a merry old time.

The French ambassador, Jean-David Levitte, came to visit me several times, and we discussed what was going on in France, including the student riots and how Chirac was handling it. It was more than just a protocol visit. He came more than once and stayed for several hours.

Ethel Kennedy came every day, and on

many occasions she brought family members, including her niece Georgeann Dowdle. She brought all sorts of food and gifts. Eunice Shriver visited and called and so did her daughter Maria, whose husband is governor of California. When Arnold Schwarzenegger called me, the first thing I said was "I want a pardon." He offered to send his private plane for me if I wanted to come work for his election in California.

Rabbi Bruce Lustig from the Washington Hebrew Congregation came in the first days of my stay at the hospice. He was one of the people we asked to be on standby for my death. He said we could have our services at his temple, and also people could stay for a reception afterward.

Word got out to the Hebrew Congregation that I had chosen their synagogue for my memorial and I had visits from the officers, who were very happy that I was going to have my service there. The rabbi stopped by a few times during the first month, but since I didn't seem to be going according to schedule, he didn't come back. On his last visit, he said to Joel, "You call me when you're ready."

The Anchormen

Tom Brokaw came to visit me many times. We are bosom buddies. Tom and I go back to when he first came to Washington to cover the White House. I was very happy to see him, because he was thinking of renting the house I owned across the street. He didn't do it, but I forgave him. I said, "I'd rather have you as a friend than a tenant."

I don't know if it was guilt for not renting my house, but Tom later put me in his book *The Greatest Generation.* People thought I was a war hero. In the piece on me he said I wasn't, but people were so impressed they made me one.

When Tom came to see me, I told him he could now write about "the Greatest Kidney," and I would send him pictures. He visited me several times with his wife, Meredith. The hospice staff was very excited. As excited as they were when Mike Wallace came to see me.

One of the nurses kept asking, "Where's Bill Clinton?" And I kept saying, "He's coming, he's coming."

Tom decided to do an interview with me for the *Today* show. He came to the hospice to film me. This was very big stuff. For his final question, he asked me what I would miss the most. I said, "Global warming."

Tom Brokaw was one of the people I asked to speak at my memorial. At first he told me he would do it for his usual fee of $30,000, plus expenses if he had to go out of town. I told him that if he did it for free, the exposure would get him a lot of paid memorial speeches. He said then perhaps he would do it for nothing. I told him he could call his address "The Greatest Generation Waiting to Die."

Another great communicator who came to visit me was Walter Cronkite. It was wonderful to see him because he is the most trusted man in America.

I never thought of Walter as an anchorman, but as a fellow I could beat at tennis. He had a sailboat on Martha's Vineyard and he kept inviting me on it. I said the reason I didn't want to go sailing with him was because the biggest lie in the world that you hear from sailors is "I'll get you back by five o'clock."

Walter came to see me with his friend Joanna Simon. She is Carly Simon's older sister, and the news she brought to me was that Carly had agreed to sing at my memorial service, but since she heard I wasn't going to die she would sing to me on the Vineyard. I said, "Tell her I want one song: 'I'll Be Seeing You (in all the old familiar places).' "

Walter and I have a deal, which is that we can't put all the plaques we have received over the years from organizations like the ACLU, the Kidney Foundation, and Hadassah on our walls because that would be too self-serving.

But there was nothing wrong with my putting Walter's plaques on the wall in my library, and he could put my plaques on his wall.

When Walter came to visit me at the hospice, I said, "I received a wonderful sculpture from the Hospice Foundation, and I'll trade you."

Walter said, "How about an ashtray from the Anti-Defamation League?"

I like Walter, so I said, "It's a deal."

My Hospice Is Your Hospice

I don't look like a person who is on his way out. I don't look that way at all. In fact, the first thing everyone says to me when they walk into the living room is, "You've never looked better!"

Were I stuck in a room out of sight I wouldn't get that attention or notoriety.

When people first come into the hospice they are very wary and careful. They don't quite know how to act or talk. They don't

103

know if there's hospice etiquette. Then, once they feel comfortable, they say, "Jesus Christ, there's no parking."

The thing that they say makes them the happiest is that we can still laugh together. There are things to laugh about in the hospice, as there are in every situation. When my lawyer, Bob Barnett, came to visit, I told him, "If you can get me seven million dollars for my book like you got for Hillary Clinton, I'll start dialysis."

There were people who showed up that I couldn't have cared less about. They decided if they came to see me they were doing a good deed, and they would be able to tell other people that they had seen me.

There were others that crashed the gate. They brought me gifts, toys, soup, coffee cake, and anything else that would make them feel welcome.

I couldn't turn them away.

One lady, Pam Gregory, brought me computer printouts of every single item that came up about me in a Google search. Some of the gifts were crazy. My doctor gave me a stuffed iguana. My three-year-old grandson brought a brightly colored stuffed grouper fish all the way from the Virgin Islands.

Other people gave me paintings and sculpture. I was tempted to open an account with eBay.

Photographs were also a very popular gift, particularly if they were pictures from some time in my past. I pasted many of them on the walls in my hospice room. Several were of lady friends, and each one thought her photo should have the prime location on my wall.

There were jokes among the hospice help about who was my favorite girlfriend. Because of the situation I had put myself in, the women really couldn't show jealousy — at least not to me.

The ladies still kept coming back and their photos kept filling up the walls.

People couldn't believe I was having so much fun.

The word spread that if you want a good time, go to the Washington Hospice.

11
MAIL CALL

The longer I stay in my hospice, and the more media coverage I get, the more mail I receive. Here are some of the questions people ask:

QUESTION: Why are you in a hospice?

ANSWER: To die with dignity, when I'm supposed to die. When I came here I was supposed to say goodbye to the world in two or three weeks. But I'm still here after nine weeks.

QUESTION: What went wrong?

ANSWER: Nobody knows — not even the doctors. It's fun to see a doctor who doesn't know what's wrong with you. Or why you're still around.

QUESTION: I've seen you on television and you seem to be very happy. Aren't you supposed to be sad?

ANSWER: I'm happy because I'm still here. I never knew how many perks were involved with dying. I have to be honest; I've enjoyed every moment of it.

QUESTION: What do you do in the hospice?

ANSWER: I spend my time on the telephone and socializing with my friends who come here every day at every hour. My mantra is "I've put death on hold." They not only visit me, and are very kind, but they also bring me food — cheesecake, shrimp, candy, cookies, and takeout from restaurants. I accept it all, even though I think there's a lot of guilt involved with people who are worrying that I'm not going to get enough to eat. The more I've been interviewed, the more friends show up to visit me. And people in town greet each other now by saying, "Have you been to the hospice yet?"

QUESTION: Do you have plans yet for your memorial service?

ANSWER: Yes, I've chosen my speakers. I showed the list to a lady friend, and she said, "You have no women speaking for you." I told her all my girlfriends are going to be pallbearers. When I mentioned it to one lady friend she became excited and asked, "What should I wear?"

■ ■ ■ ■

QUESTION: Would you recommend living in a hospice to others?

ANSWER: Not unless you can be assured you're going to be on television and in *The New York Times.* You don't want to leave this world without anybody knowing you've been here.

I was having such a good time with all this attention, I couldn't tell people any bad stories about dying. Instead, all of them were upbeat, and people told me they loved talking to someone who wasn't afraid to discuss death. Many letters said the same thing: People just wouldn't discuss death because of the unknown and fear associated with it.

Some people wrote that they believed in a hereafter, and that they would see their loved ones again in heaven. Other people insisted that the day you die it is all over. In both cases, I figured the funeral homes were the winners.

I've always been an upbeat person. It's the thing that has kept me going all my life. To the many people who wrote me, I mostly answered like this: "Thanks for your letter.

I'm writing as fast as I can. Love, Art."

Many of the letter writers said they were praying for me. If God was listening to the prayers about me, I thought, how busy could God be?

I heard from people of all faiths. People were lighting candles for me. One man told me he had planted a tree in my honor in Israel.

People sent prayer beads and even crucifixes that had been blessed. I received a beautiful watercolor painting of an angel.

I also received religious tracts. One lady in particular kept sending me cards with prayers on them. The letters proved to me that America is still close to God and that people use Him to help someone in trouble.

The big fun for me is that I've received letters from everyone you could possibly imagine, particularly when people thought I wasn't going to be around for very much longer. I had an e-mail from their majesties King Father Norodom Sihanouk and Queen Mother Monineath of Cambodia hoping for my "speedy recovery." The message came from Pyongyang, Democratic People's Republic of Korea (a.k.a. North Korea), where the couple was living due to political uncertainty in Cambodia. Unbeknownst to me, the queen has been a fan of mine since the seventies.

William F. Buckley, Jr., and I have had a correspondence over many years. Most of it has been very serious, such as why does he get a Hertz platinum membership card and I don't? I have complained many times to the CEO of Hertz. I maintained that I am syndicated in more newspapers than Buckley is, but the Hertz people didn't care. They made me stand in line.

When Bill heard that I was going to take a dirt nap he wrote me a very sympathetic letter and mentioned that Hertz might throw in six pallbearers for free. It was one of the most touching offers anyone had ever made me and eliminated one of the major expenses of my funeral. If Brokaw would speak for free and Buckley threw in my pallbearers, it would save my estate a lot of money.

Garry Trudeau was as unhappy as anybody when I told him I was in a hospice and about to buy the farm. He told me losing a leg was one thing, but losing all of me is not in the cartoon strip. Rather than being too sympathetic to my problems, he told me about his kidney stone. And then, as a friend, I told him about mine.

I wrote to him,

A kidney stone is the worst thing to have because you wish you were dead. I produced a lot of them until I had a prostate operation, and I can't tell you how great it is to be able to take a pee and not have to worry about stones.

I've done a lot of fundraising for the Kidney Foundation. To raise money I told people only if they contributed to the kidney fund would we give them Demerol. I'm sure you know about all those machines that crush stones. I worry about you now more than you should worry about me. Dying is nothing compared to passing a stone.

My dear friend Russell Baker sent me the most poignant letter of all after I wrote to him that I was not going to live.

He wrote:

Dear Art,

You have always been an impossible act to follow. Now you are writing letters that are impossible to answer. I think a lot about my own mortality, but it's just the usual dull stuff that nobody wants to hear about. You on the other hand turn it into a meditation worthy of Cicero on confronting life's heaviest burdens.

Anyhow, you've managed to get people speaking well of you. I phoned David Halberstam and Bud Trillin yesterday, and both told me what an extraordinarily "generous" person you are. I figure this means they heard you once did a free lecture for the Starving Widows and Orphans of Sri Lanka. Halberstam also used the words "gentle" and "warmth," which are the kind of words Karl Rove uses about people he plans to destroy.

Art, do you remember the time we went to Berkeley to do a program at UCal with Groucho Marx? Groucho didn't show. Had flu or bellyache or something. A million rebellious college kids had turned out, most of them to see Groucho Marx, I assumed. I figured we'd be pelted to death with spiral notebooks when we took the stage — especially me, since I had no material worth doing, figuring that Groucho would carry the show.

Fortunately, you *had* prepared something, and it was terrific. Brought the house down, in fact. I later figured you saved my life that night. I also understood why Groucho stayed home that night. He already knew you were an impossible act to follow.

Greeting Cards

Two main ways that Americans communicate with each other are by cell phone and greeting card. Over the past few weeks in the hospice I've been receiving more greeting cards than cell phone calls. It gives me a chance to study one of the largest industries in America. I am also learning about the habits of greeting card consumers.

I have received every kind of card, including "Happy Birthday." Still, the ones that I get the biggest kick out of, since I'm in a hospice, are the "Get Well" cards. Even now, some people just haven't figured out what I'm doing here.

According to the Greeting Card Association, the average person receives more than twenty cards per year. The average price of a card is two to four dollars. But if you want the card to talk, it's going to cost you ten bucks.

People send greeting cards because they save the time of writing a letter. Hallmark will do it for you. Some people feel obligated to send you a funny card — no matter how much trouble you're in. They not only send you the card, but then they call you up to find out if you got it. And if you don't react the way they expect you to, they are hurt.

Some time ago I was in Kansas City and I visited the Hallmark campus. There were several buildings, and I was given a tour. I asked, "Where are the funny cards written?" The person showing me around said, "We have a special building for them, and no one else can enter it." I walked by, hoping to hear laughter, but there was dead silence. My guide said, "They have no sense of humor."

For me, the typical card I receive has no printed message — just a pretty picture on the front and blank inside where the sender can write his own note. This takes a lot of creativity, particularly when sending a card to someone in a hospice.

The most difficult cards are those signed with only a first name, like Joan, Mary, or Susan. The senders assume they are the only Joan, Mary, or Susan you know. To make sure you're perplexed, they don't write a return address on the envelope.

Of course postage plays a big role in greeting cards. The price of a stamp keeps going up all the time. It's now thirty-nine cents, but it's still cheaper than buying a gallon of gas.

Greeting card companies are constantly thinking up new holidays or occasions to motivate people to buy cards. You have Administrative Professionals Day (formerly Secretaries Day), Grandmothers Day, Sisters-in-law Day. There are even cards that you can send when you want to break up with your lover.

Eighty percent of card buyers are women. But here's a fact: Women are more likely to buy several cards at once than men (though men generally spend more on a single card than women). The most popular cards are birthday cards, which represent 60 percent of all cards purchased, but there is still a big market for sympathy cards.

I don't expect to receive any valentines, but it would be nice if I were still around to get Christmas cards.

People ask me what I'm doing with all the cards that have been sent to me. I put them in a shoebox and they become part of my estate.

12
Poster Boy

If you stay in a hospice long enough, as I have, you can become a poster boy. I have been a poster boy for the Marine Corps, adoption, stroke, depression, kidneys, and now hospice.

This takes up a lot of my time, particularly if people aren't sure you are going to be around too long.

This is how it works: You get a call and you're asked by a friend to be the honored guest at a hospice fundraising dinner. You agree to the invitation because your friend is on the board of directors. Or you have a friend who has a friend who is on the board of directors.

You are told all you have to do is show up for the event.

What they don't tell you is that it's not that easy. You are expected to buy tables for the event and to get friends to buy tables. If the tables aren't sold, you're not considered much of a poster boy.

Okay. The first thing that goes out is the "save the date" notice, and they want the names and addresses of all your best friends. The nearer you get to the event, the more pressure is put on you to get people to buy tables.

The chairman of the dinner calls you up and says, "The tables aren't moving. We thought you would be a draw, but we were wrong. Would you buy ten tables so that we don't look silly? This is how we suggest you do it. We'll have a cocktail party at the board chairman's house. We will serve hors d'oeuvres and drinks. Nobody can leave the house unless they sign up for a table or promise to get someone else to come."

The flower committee chairwoman submits her budget. Each table must have two dozen roses. She's very proud she's getting ten percent off from her cousin who is in the business.

You get a call from the advertising chairman. He says, "No one is buying ads for the program. Would you take twelve pages and we'll print your picture as well as the members of your family?"

You have no choice except to buy the pages.

There's a special section of tables next to

the guest of honor for the "Friends of Hospice."

The dinner chairman tells you, "In order to make the dinner a sure success, we can get Tony Bennett at $250,000 for the night."

Then there is the final pre-dinner meeting. The caterer, the ballroom manager, and the pastry chef all hand in their budgets. It will cost $250,000 for the dinner, and with any luck the hospice will break even.

But it's a chance to be the poster boy for hospice. And to make it more festive, you'll get a Life Achievement Award.

The trouble is, as soon as you're finished being a poster boy for hospice, someone wants to make you Man of the Year for Frozen Shoulder Syndrome. And if that works out they offer you the Arthritis Foundation Freedom Award.

I don't know how many awards Mark Twain received in his life, but I think I'm getting close to his record.

If it weren't for the honor I wouldn't want to be the poster boy for hospice.

13
COMMUNICATION

I found out that in a hospice, communication is very important. This thought came to me when a friend of mine, Bobbie Smith, said that everyone has a private line to God, and if nobody answers at the other end, you have another day to live.

Communication is very helpful when you are dying. If you have communication, both parties feel good. But if the patient has lost his ability to communicate, it's a very frustrating thing. It's terrible for family and friends if the patient is in a coma. Then you are told to talk to them as if they are hearing you.

My family was told if I went into a coma to pretend that I was listening to them.

I remember that when Joe Kennedy, Sr., had a severely disabling stroke, all the people in the family talked to him even though he couldn't respond. Once when I went in to see him in Hyannis Port, Bobby

Kennedy told me to be sure to talk to him as if he heard everything I said. I believed I had gotten through to him when I talked to him about politics and world affairs.

In the hospice there are some patients with whom I communicate. They talk about my business and I talk about theirs.

Even when I thought it was the very end, I could make people laugh, tell jokes and stories. Friends and acquaintances that haven't seen me here in the hospice want information from those who have.

"Did you see him?"

"How was he?"

"Did he make any sense?"

"How much more time does he have?"

"I'd love to go see him, but I'm afraid I'd cry."

"Who do I call to get permission to see him?"

"He'll have to see me if I bring him something."

"I hear he prefers food to flowers."

"I haven't seen him in a long time. Do you think he'll think it's strange that I want to see him now?"

"I intended to see him last week, but I was very busy doing my taxes."

Instead of food or flowers, some people bring me terrible jokes. One of my doctors is an excellent physician, but he's no stand-up comic. Whenever he tells me a joke I always reply, "Keep your day job."

I love gossip, and if somebody brings me gossip they are very welcome. The benefit of it is that when one person gives me gossip I'm able to pass it on to someone else. So everybody prospers.

If people have children, they want to tell me all about them. Every parent I know has a story. And almost every parent has to tell it to someone. They are either bragging about their child's accomplishments or bemoaning some trouble the kid got into.

We also discuss news we read in the paper that day, news on television, and books we either love or hate. I believe the one that we have discussed the most is *The Da Vinci Code.* People all had opinions on it and they were anxious to come here and tell me their views.

One of the ways I make people happy is to tell them how much I enjoyed the dish they brought me. I ask for the recipe and then I give it to another person so they can also make it for me. I don't know whether I'm violating people's cooking rights or not.

Someone asked me once whether I talk differently to the women than to the men who come to visit. Possibly, but I've always spoken differently to women. This was true long before I was in a hospice.

I flirt more with women than with men — and always have. I like to think one of my strengths is flirting. Even in the hospice, women love to be flirted with.

When it comes to men, the hospice is like a locker room. We tell jokes.

I've listened to the play-by-play of more golf games than ever before in my life. The reason for this is I am a captive audience. I know every golf score of George Stevens, and Dave Wolper, my buddy, sends me his scores by e-mail. I now know what happened to Jack Valenti on the fifteenth hole of Burning Tree. They all mean well.

Since people in a hospice are typically senior citizens, most of the male visitors are golfers, and when you talk to them, one of the questions they ask you is, "Do you think there are any good golf courses in heaven — where women can play as well?"

I don't know the answer to this question because I'm not a golfer. In fact, hearing about somebody's game of golf is more painful than going to the dentist.

Of course there are times when you get wiped out and you want your visitors to go away. I start yawning, and if I'm lucky they say, "I think I'd better go."

Others say, "I'll just stay for a few minutes," and they wind up staying for an hour.

The toughest visitors are the ones who fly in from California, Arizona, and Florida to see you "before you go." Since they went to all the trouble to come this far (some of them even used frequent flyer miles), you have to pay them a lot of attention.

Then there are those who don't seem to realize they are in a hospice. My friend Ralph Davidson came for what I thought was a pleasant visit. After about eight minutes he started pitching me for a donation to his favorite candidate's campaign for the D.C. mayoral election.

When I told him I can't donate to political campaigns, he complained, "It's not your kidneys that don't work — it's your heart."

When he wouldn't stop, I told him, "This is worse than the physical therapy for my artificial leg."

Some visitors are only interested in my medical condition.

"How are the kidneys?"

"Are they better or worse than before?"

"What is the doctor's prognosis?"

"If you had it to do over again, would you take dialysis?"

My reply to that is, "If I took dialysis you

wouldn't be here visiting me today. And by the way, I wouldn't be here either."

14
DEATH IN THE AFTERNOON

When I'm not receiving guests I have time to watch movies from Blockbuster and think about the end.

We live and die by the movies. We may not know it, but we all imitate the roles of the actors and actresses on the screen.

I first started playing my death scenes when I went to the Saturday afternoon movies as a kid. I'd leave the theater clutching my stomach, like the gangster of the week.

One scene that I act out in my mind is Marlon Brando's final scene in *The Godfather.* Brando is playing with his grandson in the garden, and suddenly he drops dead. Even though he wasn't a good guy in the film, he died with dignity. People cry during that scene. I like to pretend I am Don Vito Corleone, going out like a great Sicilian.

There are other death scenes from films that I cherish, such as in *The Petrified Forest* when Humphrey Bogart shoots Leslie

Howard and then in turn is shot to death himself by police.

Then there's *Dead End*, when Baby Face Martin (Bogart again) is shot to death by police when he opens fire on them, after first being shot by Joel McCrea and falling from a fire escape.

I know I go back in time for my death scenes. In *The Roaring Twenties*, Bogart is pumped with lead three times by James Cagney. You are probably surprised that some of my fantasies have to do with violence, but I love to make believe that someone is going to get me, like in *High Sierra*, when I pretend I'm Humphrey Bogart and I'm picked off by a police sharpshooter.

This one has always been a favorite of mine: I pretend I'm Charles Bronson in *The Magnificent Seven*. During the final battle with the bandits I'm shot in the stomach as I lead some children to safety. I bravely die while talking to the children. A hero.

When I run out of those scenes I always go back to George Raft in *Scarface*. Raft is shot to death by Paul Muni when Muni finds Raft with Ann Dvorak.

This sounds bloody, but every once in a while I think of myself as George Raft in another of his films, *Some Like It Hot*, being shotgunned when a hit man jumps out of a cake during a banquet. If that doesn't work for me I pretend I'm Raft when he accidentally shoots himself with a backward-firing gun in *Casino Royale.*

I know some people don't think of me as the Alec Guinness type in *The Bridge on the River Kwai,* when he gets killed blowing up the bridge. This takes a lot of fantasizing because I have to wait until the bridge is built before I can blow it up.

Another favorite is the death scene in *Bonnie and Clyde.* I play Clyde to Faye Dunaway's Bonnie. I die with class.

I still think of Ronald Reagan. My favorite Reagan role is in the classic film *Knute Rockne, All American.* He is on his deathbed, and he says to Pat O'Brien, who plays Rockne, "Tell them to go out there with all they've got and win just one for the Gipper" — except I change it to "win just one for Buchwald."

I have always depended on movies to write my personal script.

I can't get the scene out of my head when I play Frank Sinatra in *From Here to Eternity* and I'm dying in Monty Clift's arms after a beating in the stockade. What makes it so endearing is that Monty Clift plays "Taps."

I like the idea of someone playing "Taps" in my final scene.

15
AWARDS FOR
STAYING ALIVE

There have been a lot of highlights here in the hospice. One of the biggest was when the French decided to award me the Order of Arts and Letters, the Legion of Honor for writers. I think it had something to do with my birthday party and that they finally wanted to acknowledge that I spent fourteen years in France.

A ceremony was held at the hospice and fifty of my friends showed up. The ambassador, Jean-David Levitte, had to get the president of France to sign off on it. The ambassador told me he was worried I wouldn't get the medal before I died, so he wrote an urgent letter to the president's office telling him the state I was in. This sped up the red tape. After the official presentation by the ambassador, Joel and Tamara, my son and daughter-in-law, made me wear the medal for several days.

When I first left for France as a young

journalist, I was told to be careful because many of the French did not speak English and were only after the few American dollars I had in my sock. But I soon discovered they were no different from the merchants back home who wanted my money, too.

As the great Francophile writer James Jones once said, "The French are the French are the French." It kept me from getting angry all the time. Plus, my French was so bad I was never sure what they were saying. I did get mad, though, at a retired French general who was the landlord of my apartment on the rue Monceau back in 1954. He was a four-star anti-Semite. Every time he saw me he would stop and say something nasty about the "Juifs."

Not wanting to lose the apartment, I would say, "Very interesting." Under my breath I said, "Fuck you." I hated that man and still do, not because of what he was, but because I didn't have enough nerve to tell him, "Fuck you, *mon général.*"

Beyond the general, I never experienced anti-Semitism, though France is rife with it. After all, they believe the Jews killed Christ. The reason I didn't feel much of it, except from the general, is the French thought of me as an American, not someone of Jewish descent.

My life in Paris centered around the European edition of the *Herald Tribune.* I landed my job in 1949, met my wife there, covered the world for the paper, and pretended to be Hemingway. In the beginning I sold myself as the food and wine critic, although I knew nothing about either. When the editor asked for my credentials, I replied, "I was a food taster in the Marine Corps."

I was arrested in 1958 when I ran through the streets of Paris with Beaux-Arts students wearing nothing but gold paint and a jockstrap. I was thrown in a jail cell at the Grand Palais. The students in the jail told the police I was a high official with the Marshall Plan, and if they didn't let us go I would take their bicycles away from them.

If you ask me to name my biggest moment in Paris, it was when four French generals staged a mutiny in Algiers against de Gaulle. At that time the Foreign Legion was made up of defrocked Nazis and storm troopers. De Gaulle had no regular troops in France, and the big fear was that the Foreign Legion from North Africa would overthrow the French government. The people were asked to drive or walk to Orly Airport and talk the Legion out of opposing de Gaulle.

My friend, Alain Bernheim, said he wasn't going because he didn't speak German.

I was on de Gaulle's side against the traitors. But revolution or no revolution, the *Herald Tribune* had to print. The mutiny failed, and de Gaulle held a lifelong grudge against his generals.

I invented myself as a journalistic Charlie Chaplin, and the more trouble I could get into, the happier I was. I made fun of the "International Set." Thornton Wilder once told me in Saint Moritz, "Archie, these people need you more than you need them. You validate their existence."

During my fourteen years in Paris I reported from Hong Kong, Algiers, Russia, Italy, and the Arctic Circle. The *Tribune* paid my expenses, or I took a junket from a movie company. I adopted my son Joel while covering *Moby Dick* in Ireland, my daughter Connie in Spain when I covered *The Pride and the Passion* with Frank Sinatra, Cary Grant, and Sophia Loren, and my daughter Jennifer in France, which I charged to Audrey Hepburn and Gary Cooper.

I am coming to the story of how I met my wife.

Ann McGarry was from Warren, Pennsylvania. She was the fashion coordinator at Neiman Marcus in Dallas, Texas, and decided to go to Paris with a thousand dollars and a letter from Stanley Marcus to the

132

couturier Pierre Balmain.

When I met her, I had been dating a fashion writer from *The Philadelphia Inquirer.* Ann had come up to her room at the Plaza Athénée to meet a moneychanger who would convert dollars into francs at a black market rate.

The next time I saw Ann was on the Champs Elysées at a café. I bought her a Pernod and she told me she lived with a French family in the Bastille area. She said they were away for the weekend.

"Okay," I said. "You can make dinner for me tomorrow night. I'll bring the wine."

To show her I was a good guy I took her home in a taxi — which cost a bundle of francs.

The next evening I showed up with a bottle of cheap Algerian red. We had dinner by candlelight. Then, thanks to the wine, we started grappling with each other on the couch. That night our friendship was consummated. We started dating, but the taxi meters kept cranking up. At the time I was living on the fifth floor of 24 rue Boccador, off Avenue George V, in a one-room studio. Irwin Shaw and Theodore White had large apartments on the other floors.

The room next to mine was up for rent, and I talked Ann into moving in. My reasoning was that after we made love I would not have to send her home in a taxi.

Ann moved in. Our rooms were connected by a balcony, and occasionally when she got mad and locked me out I went out onto the balcony in nothing but my boxer shorts and a top hat and read poetry to her. There was nothing she could do but let me in.

We lived in sin for about a year, but then Ann started asking, "Isn't there anything more?"

I said, "What more can there be?"

"I want to get married."

"But that would spoil all the fun," I said.

From then on she threatened to go home unless I became serious.

I said, "I am serious, but no French priest wants to marry us because everyone thinks I killed Christ."

One night a few weeks later in a bar called Calvados, where our gang gathered after dinner, the subject of marriage came up again. Lena Horne said in front of everybody, "If you want to get married I know a priest in London who will do it."

I was trapped. I said, "I'll go see him." The gang bought Ann a bottle of Champagne.

The next week I went to Westbury Cathedral in London and asked to see Father

Kennedy. "Lena Horne sent me. She said you would marry my beloved and me."

"No problem."

"But there is a problem. My wife is Catholic and I am Jewish."

He replied, "No problem, as long as you are not a Protestant."

And so we lived happily ever after for forty years.

After we got married, Ann and I found a beautiful apartment on the Quai d'Orsay and tried to make babies. In time we discovered we couldn't produce an heir. So we decided to adopt one. I have wondered many times what it would be like if Ann were still alive while I'm in the hospice. Since she always blamed herself for anything that went wrong in our lives, I'm sure she would blame herself for the state I'm in now.

In a weird way I'm glad I am going after her.

Don't Fail Me Now

Another highlight was getting the National Hospice Award from the Hospice Foundation of America. They gave it to me because I had publicized the institution.

My son, Joel, attended the awards dinner and spoke for me.

On behalf of my father, thank you very much. I have to be honest with you, we didn't want my father to go into a hospice at first. We were hoping he would stay on dialysis, but when he went off dialysis, it was his decision, and we came around to supporting him.

No one wants to lose their loved one, but when my father chose to go into hospice he seemed relieved and happy that the decision had been made.

In all the interviews and profiles, Dad has consistently talked about hospice and its purpose, which for him is to make dying respectable.

Since my father is in such good shape mentally, there is a tremendous amount of laughter in the hospice. With so many people coming to see him, he jokes about charging $25 per visit and $30 for parking.

It would not be as much fun for me to accept this award if Dad were not here. I promise that we will all send the message that when the time comes, hospice will be there for your loved ones.

As weeks turned into months, I began to wonder why I was still alive, as did everyone else, including people who had written, called, or visited expecting that it would be our last contact.

I asked Dr. Newman how I had become The Man Who Would Not Die.

This is how he recalled the situation:

After your leg amputation you seemed very sad, upset, and frustrated, which was understandable. I discussed with you the need for dialysis to do the work of your kidneys. If you didn't have it, your situation was terminal.

At first you resisted. You told me, "This is not me. This is not how I want to be."

Then you asked me what it was like to die from kidney failure. I said you will become uremic and go into a coma.

You said, "That's all right. It sounds good."

After the leg surgery you were transferred to the National Rehabilitation Hospital.

While recuperating from losing your leg you told me you were very depressed and I said, "You have a right to be, but I want to make sure you're not making decisions based on depression."

On January 15, 2006, you said to me, "I want out of here, nothing is working and I don't see any good coming of this. I've had a very good life and I just want to go out

137

peacefully."

I spoke to the family and said I was acting according to your wishes. I arranged your transfer to the Washington Home and Hospice for supportive care and no further rehabilitation or dialysis. At that time your kidneys were not functioning. Gradually the kidneys began to rally and produce urine — good quality urine in good volume. The blood tests and urine tests showed improvement. It became clear that the insult to the kidneys caused by the angiogram dye was resolving and now you no longer have both acute and chronic kidney failure, but just chronic kidney disease. If there is no further injury to your kidneys you can have a reasonable life without dialysis.

This was the best news I had received in this long medical saga. My kidneys did not let me down and did not fail me after all. If I could, I would give them a very gentle hug, as I don't want to bruise them.

16
SEX AND LIES

You're probably wondering if I give much thought to sex in the hospice. I have given it some thought, but not as much as I give to food.

One Sunday I saw a cover story in *The New York Times Magazine,* and also a piece on *60 Minutes,* about women who want children but not men. Because sperm banks are becoming more popular all the time, a man can now make a deposit at a sperm bank and the recipient can pick out what kind of baby she would like to have. (Baseball player, stand-up comedian, White House aide.) Sperm banks have become so sophisticated that mothers can select the color of their baby's hair, eyes, and so on. When I saw both of these stories on Sunday, I decided it was a sign. Why not me? This would be a wonderful way to achieve immortality.

The following Monday I called the sperm bank in California and asked where I could leave a deposit. They said, "We're always open to new accounts. We will send you a specimen jar and put you in our computer. Then you tell us how many women you'll allow to receive your donation. If, for example, you would like to make a lot of women happy, you would have to make more than one donation. The specimen will be frozen and good for six months."

This was a fantastic discovery, because before, I was under the impression I wouldn't be able to leave anything behind. Since reading the article, I have been sitting here dreaming about the future little Arties and Arianas running around all over the place. I can follow them in my mind to school and even dream about them going to college. The boys will then be drafted by the Washington Redskins, and if it's a girl, she'll be a Redskin cheerleader.

Believe it or not, the sperm banks pay for deposits in cash, but they don't promise you a toaster like some other banks.

Since it's my deposit, I want my offspring to go to good schools. Not necessarily Ivy League colleges, but if it's a boy, and he gets a football scholarship to USC, I think that's nice. If it happens to be a girl, and she's a champion tennis player for Sweet Briar, it is very exciting. My whole idea now is that I will not go without leaving something worthwhile for posterity. There are a lot of sperm banks in the country. I have even heard of drive-in branches.

The other thing is, I keep looking at women and wondering which one of them I want to be the mother of my child.

To make life easy for everybody, I'm putting up a website with all the relevant information on me. I do have faults, but I still think whatever they are can be overcome.

I know this is going to produce a lot of interest from single women, but I don't want them to get their hopes up. At my age I can only give twelve deposits a week.

As long as I'm in a hospice, I might as well talk about sex. There isn't much in the hospice and I can't say I had a lot before I got here.

I was fifteen years old when I lost my virginity to a chambermaid at the Hotel Nassau in Long Beach, Long Island, in 1941. I was a bellboy. Her name was Anna (I think). I only mention it because losing my virginity was a good thing, and since it happened I have never wanted to get even with Anna or any other woman.

I believe in sex. I think it is good for you if you don't hurt anybody else. I have been hurt, not by making love, but by rejection.

Over the years I have collected rejections the way other men have collected baseball cards.

"I don't want to make love to you because it will hurt our friendship."

"You are just using me."

"I know what you are thinking, and the answer is no."

"I want to do it, but I don't want to have a baby."

"My mother said if you don't want to marry me I should keep my legs closed."

"I can't give you what you want."

"Everyone says you sleep around."

"I'm not in love with you."

"If we made love and you didn't call me the next morning I would die."

"I can't do it in a car."

I have one of the great rejection collections of the world.

I was introduced to the idea of sex when I was eleven years old. My unofficial tutor was a young man named Harold, the son of my first foster parents.

I shared a room in the attic with an Irish maid named Celeste. Once or twice a week

Harold, when drunk, came upstairs and got in bed with Celeste.

They went at it, thrashing and moaning and saying things like, "Don't stop" and "Now, now!"

Two feet separated my bed from them, so while they were screwing, I was masturbating. Harold and Celeste would look at me and laugh. Harold said, "If you don't tell my mother, I'll buy you a present."

After that, when Harold came upstairs to bang Celeste, I whacked off and then got a baseball glove, or roller skates, or a stamp collection.

My sister Doris asked me why Harold was giving me presents. I told her, "Because he likes me."

Once I was introduced to masturbation at the age of eleven, it became one of my favorite indoor and outdoor sports. While doing it I made "love" to my English teacher, a girl named Mitzi who worked in the dry cleaner's down the block, and a slew of movie stars.

Whenever I saw a movie at the Hollis Theater I went home and made love to the "actress of the week." Like so many boys who grew up in the thirties, I had wet dreams about Jean Harlow, Carole Lombard, and Mary Astor. For reasons I never understood, if you were caught masturbating you were punished. No one would believe me if I told them that the devil made me do it.

When I was thirteen years old, I visited Billy Mahler at his fancy prep school in Lawrenceville, New Jersey. Coming home, my plan was to hitchhike back on U.S. 1. It was six o'clock in the evening. Cars kept whizzing by. Finally a man in a fancy Buick stopped for me. I remember every detail.

He was wearing a checked sports jacket, a dark blue shirt, and a red striped tie. He asked me where I went to school and what my favorite sport was.

Then he asked if I liked women. I said I did. He told me he was a traveling salesman and sold kitchenware and met a lot of women. As a matter of fact, he had just made love to a waitress in a Howard Johnson in Maryland the night before.

He didn't leave it at that. He told me what beautiful breasts she had and how she performed oral sex on him. While he gave me the details I could feel his hand on my crotch. He saw I had an erection.

I was scared silly, but U.S. 1 saved me. It had traffic lights. When we stopped at a red light in New Brunswick, New Jersey, I jumped out of his car and ran into the bushes, where I hid for an hour.

I never knew his name, but I have hated him all my life — and I avoid traveling on U.S. 1, although I never told anyone the reason why.

I don't want you to think I have only liked sex for sex's sake. When I was married I tried to make babies, but to no avail. I would even rush home in the middle of the day, we would make love, but nothing would happen. I enjoyed sex in the afternoon, particularly since it was for a purpose.

I remember my first real love mainly because she dumped me. Flossie Starling, a Southern magnolia, gave her heart to me and then took it away. It was the summer of 1942 at the Mount Washington Hotel in New Hampshire. She was a waitress and I was a bellboy. We pledged eternal love and did some very heavy petting after dark on the eighteenth hole of the golf course.

Flossie went to the University of North Carolina at Greensboro. I lied and told her I was going to Columbia. The summer whizzed by and I was sure our love was forever. Flossie promised she would wait for me until I finished "law" school.

I wasn't very happy to return to Forest Hills. My sisters and I lived in an upstairs three-room apartment. But we had no furniture, because we couldn't afford any. I couldn't let anyone upstairs. Neither could my sisters.

I hated school. It is a crazy thing to say, but World War II saved me. I decided to run away and join the Marines. They had beautiful uniforms, and in the movies, when they weren't fighting the Japs, the Marines were fighting U.S. dogface soldiers and sailors in bars.

One Monday I left home quietly and headed south to say goodbye to Flossie in Greensboro. My family had no idea where I was going. All the way hitchhiking down to Greensboro, I dreamed of my farewell with Flossie: She would hold me in her arms and cry when she found out I was going to fight in the malaria-infested jungles of Guadalcanal.

I arrived at Flossie's dorm on Friday afternoon. When she came downstairs she failed to throw her arms around me. Instead, she asked angrily, "What are you doing here?"

It turned out that Flossie had a boyfriend, a cadet at the Virginia Military Academy, with whom she had a date that night. Flossie didn't know what to do with me, so she set me up with her roommate Sylvia.

The four of us went out dancing and I had a terrible night. Sylvia didn't care for me and I only had eyes for Flossie. The other three were furious when I didn't have money to pay for food after the dance. They dropped me off at the YMCA and didn't say good night.

The next morning, Saturday, I decided I had no choice but to join the Marine Corps. The recruiting office was in the post office and it closed at noon. When I walked in, the sergeant looked at me and asked, "How old are you?"

I said, "Seventeen."

He said, "You have to have your parents' consent."

"No problem. My dad is in town now buying feed."

He said, "And the permission papers have to be notarized."

"I gotcha."

I left the post office, which was next to skid row. While I was trying to figure things out, a grizzled old man came up to me and said, "Mister, can I have a dime for a drink?"

I said, "I will give you a half pint of Southern Comfort if you do something for me."

"What's that?" he asked.

"I want you to be my father for an hour

147

so I can enlist in the Marine Corps."

The old man said, "Why, that's patriotic."

We found a notary and I told him I was trying to get into the Marines but my father had been drunk for a month and couldn't sign the papers. I asked him if I could hold "Dad's" hand while he signed.

The notary said, "I'll do anything to help our boys join the service."

Once the form was signed, I gave the Southern Comfort to my "father." Then I rushed back to the post office and the sergeant swore me in. He gave me meal tickets and a bus ticket to Yamasee, South Carolina, the departure point for Parris Island. I called Flossie and said, "Flossie, I am now a Marine."

She snarled, "You behaved beastly last night and I never want to see you again."

"But Flossie, I will be going overseas and I might never come back."

Flossie didn't come down to the bus station at the last moment to see me off as I dreamed she would.

There is one more blow I still carry from that time. On the bus from Greensboro to Parris Island, I was sitting in the front seat. Just after we left Raleigh, an elderly black lady (in those days we didn't use the words

African American) got on the bus. I stood up to give her my seat. The driver stopped the bus and looked at me and asked, "What are you doing?"

"I'm giving the lady my seat."

The driver just stared at me. The lady moved to the back of the bus. The passengers glared at me as if I had done something terribly wrong.

The reason I remember that bus ride so well is that it was my first experience with overt racial hate. And I have truly hated that bus driver all of my life.

In boot camp, whenever I thrust my bayonet into a target I pretended it was the driver. You can hate someone forever, even if you don't know his name.

Over the years, the hurt for Flossie mixed with fantasy. I dreamed I would come back in my dress Marine uniform (which I won in a crap game) and Flossie would come down the stairs and say, "Arthur, you are back and you are alive!" We would embrace while a string orchestra played "I'll Be Seeing You."

The truth of the matter is I never heard from her until forty years later when I was signing my memoir *Leaving Home* in Greensboro. There she was, just like it said in "I'll Be Seeing You." She was pleased I had written about her, and said, "Would you like to go to Florida with me?" I asked her, "Where were you when I needed you?"

I was home from the war to celebrate VJ Day and I went down to Broadway. Times Square was filled with thousands of people. Anyone in uniform was hugged and kissed. I didn't know how to deal with all the attention. Then I saw a liquor store and bought a pint of bad whiskey called "America the Brave." I drank it not slowly, but all at once. Then I sat down on the curb and got sick.

I don't remember anything after that until the next morning when I woke up on a couch in a Spanish lady's apartment.

As she made coffee, she explained that she had felt sorry for me, so she had taken me home to her apartment.

At that moment I became very mad at myself. I knew I would never see another VJ night, and I had wasted it in a drunken stupor.

17
IN THE NEWS

You might be wondering how I get my news in the hospice. Just like everybody else. Some days are good days, and some are bad. There was one week full of good news.

Tom DeLay announced he wasn't going to run for Congress. In one story he said he was doing God's will. Another said he could be in trouble for raising money by doing favors.

I was not joyful when I heard the news. DeLay is one of the few targets in Congress who is known by everyone. When I mention his name I don't even have to say "The Hammer." I don't know whether people enjoy reading about him because he was once an exterminator, or because as the leader of the House he took favors from Jack Abramoff.

What will the media do without Tom De-Lay? They will find somebody almost as good, although they'll have to wait for the next election.

The next story that the country enjoyed had to do with the president telling Dick Cheney a secret, which he passed on to I. Lewis Libby. The attorney general said the president had a right to leak secret stuff to the public if it's in our interest. I agreed because Bush is my president and I trust someone who is not afraid to leak classified information.

The fall guy is Libby, the vice president's aide, who passed on the information to newspaper people that former ambassador Joe Wilson's wife worked for the CIA. No one knows how the president broke the story to Cheney. I think he said, "Dick, I'm going to tell you a CIA secret. Don't tell anybody except Bob Novak, Judy Miller, or anybody else who likes to print CIA secrets."

Since Libby has not yet been tried, the story has legs and will be around for a while.

The third good story of the week came from, of all places, the *New York Post.* The newspaper has a Page Six feature that prints all the gossip that's fit and not fit to print. One of the Page Six reporters was caught trying to extort money from a billionaire. In exchange for "managing" the coverage on him, he promised not to write anything bad about the victim, Ron Burkle, for a fee of $100,000 plus $10,000 a month. Burkle, an investor in supermarkets and all sorts of businesses, blew the whistle on the gossip columnist to the FBI. They conducted a sting operation, which produced photographs, tapes, and other evidence against the reporter.

What made it such a good story is that *The New York Times* and the *Daily News* both printed it on their front pages. This was payback against Rupert Murdoch, who owns the *New York Post,* and people say Page Six is his favorite feature. What makes it an even stranger story is that the *New York Post* didn't print anything about the sting at all.

In any case, I liked the story because it had nothing to do with leaks from the White House.

My favorite story, though, was about the discovery of an ancient scroll, the Gospel of Judas. In the ancient text it turns out that Judas was a good guy and when he blew the whistle on Jesus, it was Jesus' idea.

The discovery changed a lot of people's thinking about Judas's role at the Last Supper. It now also affects people's Passover plans.

Global Warming

Tom Brokaw asked me what I'm going to miss the most when I'm gone. I told him global warming.

That got me thinking about a good way for George Bush to defend his environmental policies.

Bush's handlers point out to the president that he has not said enough about global warming lately and it is becoming a sore point with the public.

One adviser says, "Let's set up a news conference and advertise the fact that the president will talk about global warming."

The president agrees it is a good idea and asks, "Where should we hold the conference?"

Another adviser answers, "What do you think about holding a fundraiser on the Arctic Ocean?"

Someone else says, "What about on the *Titanic?*"

"And we'll have a big banner saying MISSION ACCOMPLISHED."

The president says, "I like it. But what do I say exactly about my stand on global warming?"

"You can say that the press only writes about bad things, like the earth getting warmer and polar ice caps melting. And then you will announce that your environmental adviser, who formerly worked for the Petroleum Institute, says that scientists don't know what they're talking about."

Bush says, "I have never trusted scientists. They just stick with the numbers, and all they want to do is hurt us politically."

"Then, Mr. President, you will assure the country that the *Titanic* will never hit an iceberg as long as you're president. And even if we do, you will stay the course."

The president nods his head. "Should I talk about greenhouse gases that are melting the ice at both poles?"

"We think it's a good idea to say that although emissions may be responsible for the melting, American corporations are dependent on carbon dioxide to keep their factories going. You should also say warm weather will cut down on the use of heating oil."

The president says, "This would be a good place to attack the environmentalists."

An adviser says, "If any of the scientists try to make us look silly on global warming we'll censor their reports."

The president asks, "Can I promise we will bring the boys home by Christmas?"

"Good idea."

An adviser says, "The temperature

changes can't but help your popularity. You'll go down in history as the American president that warmed the world."

Another adviser says, "The country will remember that you were the captain of the *Titanic,* and if it weren't for you, the ship would have struck an iceberg."

"Mr. President, this will be a great photo op."

The president asks, "Who will we put on the deck of the *Titanic* to cheer me on?"

"Conservatives, antienvironmentalists, polar bears, seals, and penguins."

A Tank Full of Money

People don't know it, but there's money to be made in the oil and gasoline business. The question is, who's making the money? No one knows for sure, but the heads of the oil companies are driving away with satchels of cash in the trunks of their SUVs.

When I read in the paper that former Exxon CEO Lee Raymond received $400 million a year, I began dreaming about being the CEO of an oil company. This is how it goes for me:

Four hundred million is not a lot of money because you still have to pay for groceries, bus fare, and taxes on the windfall profits that come your way.

I ask my vice president, "How many barrels of oil did we buy today? How much did we sell? And how much is in it for us?"

He replies, "Sir, things are going okay. It could be better, because we're selling our product for only $3.90 a gallon."

"What are the other companies charging?" I ask.

"That's the funny thing. They're charging the same price — $3.90."

"So that means they're not going to undersell us."

My vice president says, "They wouldn't dare do that, because gas companies have to stick together. There are only five of us now. And although it's not a bundle, we still have to share the wealth."

The marketing manager comes out of the men's room and says, "Sir, would you have any objection if we upped the price to four dollars a gallon?"

I say, "Well, I wouldn't if the other companies do the same thing."

"Sir, we're starting to get some flak from Congress because they say we're gouging our customers."

I reply, "It's not true. We won't be gouging them until we are at seven dollars a gallon. They'll thank us when they realize they can still drive to work without pain. By the

157

way, I want the PR people in here, because I'm sick and tired of the newspapers and TV stations using the word 'pain' when they talk about our profits. Let's take out some ads that say, 'Pain is in the eye of the beholder.' "

"Well said, sir. I haven't seen any pain on the twentieth floor since I've been here. What happens if Congress gets so nervous that they start putting pressure on us to lower the price?"

"We will say it's not the U.S., it's China. If we want to solve our problems in this country, we've got to tell China they have to use a lot less oil when they make their toys and sneakers."

The vice president says, "We will inform them that Americans have no intention of spoiling their summer vacations."

"We could also have our lobbyist declare we'll never have enough supply unless we drill for oil in polar bear country."

"What about drilling in the Gulf of Mexico?" the marketing manager asks. "Why don't we push for ten illegal Mexicans coming into the country with every barrel of oil?"

I say, "No one understands power until they run an oil company. And the beauty of it is, just because I make four hundred million a year doesn't mean I have forgotten the little guy."

My secretary comes in and says, "Your Gulfstream has just arrived at the airport and the pilot wants to know if you plan to fly to Saudi Arabia today."

18
SPOILED ROTTEN

As I was telling you: Soon after the celebration of my eightieth birthday, my right leg went out on me. There was no circulation. Dr. Christopher Attinger at Georgetown University Hospital Limb Center had no choice but to cut it off.

It is one of the saddest things I have lived with — even if Medicare was willing to pay for it. One day I had two good legs; the next day I had only one.

Nobody I know wants to lose a limb. It is a violation of the integrity of the body.

You don't give it much thought until it happens to you. Then you discover how important every part of your body is, even an ingrown toenail.

When the hospice podiatrist came to care for my remaining foot, I told him I thought I should get half price. He said, "No, it's double."

In my case the loss of a leg interfered with

walking and getting in and out of cars, and I required the assistance of other people to do the simplest things, such as getting out of bed and sitting in a chair.

The fact that my kidneys are still working made it possible for Dr. Newman to recommend that I get a prosthesis, which is an artificial leg.

Once you attach a new leg you are assigned a physical therapist. They are experts in pain and their main idea is that if there is no pain, there is no progress. I accused my therapist of being a former prison guard at Guantánamo Bay.

Here is the joke. My main problem is my kidneys, but the only thing people can see wrong with me is that I have a missing leg.

Once I made up my mind to get the leg, I decided to sell advertising space on it. I also asked people to donate money to a fund to pay for my new leg. My friend Joe Califano responded to my request in a letter:

Dear Artie:

After consulting with my attorney, I decided not to give you $1,000 towards your new leg. In fact, my attorney suggests that you probably owe me money because of a fraudulent attempt to extort $1,000 on the basis that you were dying.

If you make the contribution, I will, of course, not press charges.

Sincerely,
Joseph A. Califano, Jr.

And now for the good news.

Even though I lost my leg, there are some positive aspects about it. Everybody treats me like an invalid. I don't have to lift a finger if I want something. People keep hovering over me nervously. All I have to do is ask and people rush to accommodate me.

Example:

"What do you want for dinner?"

"I don't care."

"Would you like lobster?"

"It's expensive."

"You're worth it."

Or:

"What books do you want to read that we can buy for you? And are you happy with the videos we rented?"

I have my choice of seats at sporting events, and the most important thing of all, a handicapped parking permit.

My handicapped sign is my badge of honor. I didn't ask to have my leg removed, but since it was, I deserve decent parking.

Yes, I am spoiled rotten. People are afraid of me. They are solicitous. I love to be treated this way. I think I'm getting terribly spoiled. Friends say I'm going to have to go to remedial charm school.

I behave like Marlon Brando in *On the Waterfront.* "I could have been a contender."

The only time I'm on my best behavior is when I'm signing books.

Goodbye, leg. I didn't need you as much as I thought.

19
FIVE PEOPLE

One of my favorite recent books is *The Five People You Meet in Heaven,* by Mitch Albom. It gets one to thinking about the five people. It's a game we play at the hospice all the time, and I give it a lot of thought.

So far my list is: Ava Gardner, Grace Kelly, Marilyn Monroe, Rita Hayworth, and Judas.

I don't get much response concerning the women I would like to meet. But there is always hesitation when Judas's name comes up.

"Why Judas? And what would you say to him?"

I would ask him about his personal relationship with Jesus. Were they really good buddies, as written in the Judas Scroll? Or was he a turncoat?

The evidence for Judas being a good guy is very slim. We just have the scroll and Leonardo da Vinci's "Last Supper."

164

For centuries, when people have studied the painting, they have noticed that Judas doesn't seem to be enjoying his wine. Leonardo has twelve disciples painted at Passover, but when you look at them it's hard to decide who is the one that betrayed Jesus.

We can say what we want, but only when we meet Judas in heaven will we solve the mystery. The case for the Judas Scroll is very interesting. It reveals that Jesus *asked* Judas to betray him. In that way, Jesus could fulfill the prophecy and go to heaven to rise again.

For two thousand years Judas has been accused of being anti-Semitic. When I get to heaven I hope I can change all this. Come to think of it, I could talk Leonardo into doing a new painting. This one would be called "The da Vinci Code."

After I wrote a column about our little game of "Five People," I heard from a lot of readers who picked up on the game.

Everybody seems to have a different list of people they want to meet in heaven. Some of the most popular choices are Abraham Lincoln, Cary Grant, Napoleon, and Madame Curie.

A friend of mine, Albert Prendergast, asked me why we couldn't list the people we do *not* want to meet in heaven. He pointed out it's a game people would love to play, and, of course, the list is much longer.

Now, get a yellow legal pad and a pencil. Start writing down the names of people you don't want to meet in heaven. (You can eliminate people you don't believe would make it to heaven in the first place, for example, Adolf Hitler, Joseph Stalin, Jack the Ripper, and Al Capone.)

If you're serious about playing, it is much more fun to select people that have been involved in your life.

I'm still working on my list of the "Five People I Don't Want to Meet in Heaven." There is the USC coed who dumped me in college for a fraternity jock; the person who devised the new SAT test, making it so my grandson couldn't get into college; the lady who hijacked my parking place at the shopping mall and laughed when she got out of her car; the insurance claims adjuster who wouldn't pay for damages to my house; and the Japanese soldier whose life I spared in the South Pacific during World War II and later sold me a Honda.

Prendergast pushed the game a little farther. You not only have to list the people you do not want to meet in heaven, but also explain the things you won't do for them. For example, you would not share a golf game with them, not give them tickets to a rock concert, or, if you want to be cruel, not show up for a date you had made with the person.

If they serve drinks in heaven, the people on your list would have to pay for their own. Also, in case there are jobs in heaven, you would make sure someone on your list doesn't get a job and is not entitled to health insurance.

One of the things you have to find out when you get up there is whether the person you don't want to meet has also arrived. There is a database called "People I Don't Want to Meet in Heaven." In it you can look up names. It makes no sense to try to avoid running into people if they never got to heaven in the first place.

It's obvious that there are far more people you don't want to meet in heaven than those you do.

Another rule is that you are allowed to list only one ex-wife. For example, if your first wife is going to bug you, you have to avoid her at all costs.

The perfect game is when *your* name is on the lists of all the people you likewise don't want to meet. That is even more fun than winning at Scrabble.

Warning: If you don't want to meet someone in heaven, don't pick him up at the airport.

While we're on the subject of going to heaven, there's another game we play.

QUESTION: If you had only six months to live, how would you spend them?

I've asked several friends the question. Two said they would like to spend their last months with their children. And one said, "I don't even know where my children are."

Another friend said, "If I had only six months to live I'd go to Las Vegas and put up a million dollars at Binion's poker table."

One lady said she'd go to Prada and get a decent pair of shoes. "You can't walk around in loafers for six whole months."

A male friend said he would watch every basketball final from courtside.

There was one man who was very surly, and he said that he would spend his last months getting even with all the people who had been mean to him. What makes him a real sourpuss is that he said, "There is no one in heaven I want to meet — I might not even want to go there. If a doctor tells me I have only months to live, I'll get a second opinion."

AFTERWORD: TOO SOON TO SAY GOODBYE

This is the first day of my life, after nearly five months of living in the hospice.

The purpose of the hospice is to help you pass away gently when all else fails. You are supposed to do it with as little pain as possible and with dignity.

It didn't work out that way for me.

In spite of the fact that I've been staying in a hospice, I'm not going to heaven immediately. My doctor informs me that I can stop over on Martha's Vineyard on the way there.

For many months I have been waiting to go quietly into the night.

For reasons that even the doctors can't explain, my kidneys kept working, and what started out as a three-week deathwatch turned into five months of living, eating, and laughing with my friends.

The more publicity I got, the more attention my kidneys got, and so instead of going quietly into the night, I was holding press conferences every day.

Since I was expected to die soon, the French ambassador gave me the literary equivalent of the Legion of Honor.

Because of the publicity I had gotten, the National Hospice Association made me their Man of the Year.

I have had such a good time at the hospice. I am going to miss it.

I never realized dying could be so much fun.

Then a few weeks ago my doctor said I had to change course. He advised me to go to Martha's Vineyard instead. So that's where I am now.

Things that I had stopped caring about because I was going to die, I now had to start caring about again. This included shaving in the morning and buying a new cell phone that works. I had to rewrite my living will and scrap all the plans for my funeral. I also had to start worrying about Bush again.

But I'm glad to be back on Martha's Vineyard. The Vineyard is part of my life and has been for the last forty-five years. In the early sixties, I rented a house from the town dentist. After five years of renting different places, I finally bought my own home on Main Street in Vineyard Haven. The house is on what we call "Writers' Row," because John Hersey, Bill Styron, Mike Wallace, Lillian Hellman, and others have lived there.

I am surprised but happy to have the chance to say, "You can take me out of the Vineyard, but you can't take the Vineyard out of me."

Over the past months, many people have asked me, "What is it like to die?" I've had to answer, "I don't know, because I haven't died. I thought I was going to, but things have changed."

Alas, the people who come to visit me now look at me with great suspicion. They want to know if the whole thing was a scam. They can't believe after I said goodbye that I wound up on Martha's Vineyard instead of going to paradise.

I called up the TV stations and the newspapers and asked them if they would make a correction and retract the original story. They said they never correct stories about people who claimed they were dying and didn't.

So, this is where I am now. I'm still seeing friends, but instead of saying farewell, we discuss what the Redskins are going to do.

I don't know how long I'll be around on Martha's Vineyard. But if nothing else, I know I made an awful lot of people happy.

So, dear reader, I hope you don't feel you were duped. The moral of this story is, never trust your kidneys.

EPILOGUE

I planned my death very carefully and was quite concerned about my memorial service. I asked eight people to be my pallbearers and they all accepted.

Then I remembered that if I died I couldn't hear myself being eulogized, so I got the idea to print their eulogies at the end of my book. Instead of being memorialized after my death, I get to read what they were going to say now. It's very rare that someone has the chance to hear his own eulogies.

March 11, 2006

To: Tom Brokaw, Mike Wallace, Ben Bradlee, George Stevens, Jr., Ken Starr, Dr. Michael Newman

My dear comrades in arms,
    You have been chosen by Publishers

Clearinghouse to be one of the speakers at my memorial celebration. I can't give you a date, but whenever it is, we're going to have a celebration at the Washington Hebrew Congregation on Macomb Street.

The date will be about ten days to two weeks after I'm gone. We're planning on a 7:00 p.m. starting time. While I can't give you an exact date, I can tell you how long we'd love you to speak. I think three minutes would be a perfect amount of time to tell me how wonderful I am. This is not a joke. I would love you to be a speaker at my memorial celebration.

Please RSVP to this letter if I'm still here. If not, tell Joel. He and Jennifer will be speaking for the family. The rest of you are dear friends.

Love and kisses,

Art

By Tom Brokaw

We all know how Art valued his friends, that he was generous to them, thoughtful and, to the very end, protective of their best interests and reputation. It was in that spirit that he authorized me to disclose here that he arranged for and financed ghostwriters for the eulogies submitted by Mike Wallace, George Stevens, and Ben Bradlee.

The touching sentiments, witty construction, and evocative memories are all very nice, and certainly worthy of the occasion. But they were bought, paid for, and edited by Artie.

As he explained the arrangement to me, it wasn't just that Mike, George, and Ben needed the help, although that was a concern. He said if his memorial ever became a movie, he wanted his estate to own the rights. "Look," he said, "I already got a book out of dying. Why not a movie? And this time I don't want to sue for my share."

I was excused from the ghostwriter exercise because I had already written how he was the greatest Marine of his generation, a fearless and highly decorated editor and publisher of a one-page mimeographed South Pacific newsletter, an assignment he received after dropping a bomb while attempting to load it onto an airplane.

Art won the war and then came home and conquered the world.

His loyal subjects stretched from the sunny pathways of USC to Parisian boulevards, from the nation's capital to Manhattan's canyons and Vineyard beaches to every home with a newspaper and every lecture hall with an adoring audience.

As Meredith and I ascended through the layers of life in Los Angeles, Washington, and New York, family and friends back in the Midwest were not much impressed — until Artie started using our names as part of the cast of characters in his column.

Now, that was validation.

He loved his celebrity but he wore it lightly, like one of those odd hats or garish jackets he was so fond of. To walk through an airport or into a restaurant with Artie was never a private matter. "Hi, how are ya?" he greeted everyone.

He just *knew* everyone wanted to say hello, and he was right. One night in Florida, patrons at a popular restaurant, most of them Jewish and Art's age, hit the lottery: Buchwald and George Burns at side-by-side tables.

I'm not sure if George and Art had met before, but it didn't matter. They got along famously. After all, they belonged to the same club. They were once poor and obscure but they always loved to make people laugh. It wasn't just that they made people laugh. They had such a good time doing it.

That made them rich, famous — and beloved.

Everyone in that restaurant went home that night thinking they had spent the evening with two old friends.

Art was best known for his column and books, but his other genius was on the lecture circuit, a sideline so lucrative I once called it "white collar crime," to his dismay.

His appearances defied all the rules of public oratory. He'd amble to the podium clutching a fistful of three-by-five cards filled with topical one-liners and begin to read them one by one, pausing only to join in the roars of laughter as he nailed one punch line after another. It was never clear who enjoyed his humor more, Art or his audience.

He owned the audience, except one time during President Reagan's first term when Art was having sport with the Gipper before a high-powered business group. There were some grumbles. Art picked up the mood of the room and said, "Okay, how many of you here will vote to re-elect Ronald Reagan?" Every hand went up, defiantly.

Art grinned and then said, "And how many of you here would hire Ronald Reagan to run your company?"

There was a stunned silence and then gales of laughter.

Art was always on, but never tiresome. And he transcended generations. During visits to San Francisco he'd call our daughter Andrea, then a Berkeley student, and invite her to dinner with friends, fellow humorists Art Hoppe and Herb Caen, all men old enough to be her grandfather. She'd show up in her Cal student wardrobe and laugh all night long.

Uncle Artie was just that to the children of his friends and whenever he appeared before student audiences. In his many commencement speeches, Art liked to tell the graduates, with great mocking solemnity, "We have given you a perfect world. Don't screw it up."

He has given his friends, their families, and his audiences so many laughs and so much joy through the years that that alone would be an enduring legacy. But Art was never just about the quick laugh. His humor was a road map to essential truths and insights that might otherwise have eluded us.

Over the years I've "borrowed" Art's best

lines for my own use. I cherished those dinners and lunches when he would hold forth about the foibles of politicians and even friends. I never tired of the stories of those days in Paris. (I once asked when he knew it was time to leave there and return to the U.S. He said the night Sinatra called and wanted to go out and Art made up an excuse to stay in.)

But I've never had a richer appreciation of his friendship and presence among us than during the final passage of his life, when, facing death, he taught us anew lessons in courage, grace, friendship, family, and the mysteries of the human body, laughing all the way.

In turn, Art, we have given you a perfect sendoff.

Don't screw it up.

By Mike Wallace

The individual at issue is, plain and simple, a fraud, a publicity-seeking, lying, greedy fraud. Greedy enough to ask his old friends to sign his new prosthetic leg at a thousand dollars a clip, and we damn fools are lining up to do it.

Truth is, he used to be genuinely sick: bad kidney, couldn't pee, didn't want to bother with dialysis because it was too boring, didn't want an organ transplant — he was too content at the prospect of dying.

I remember his phone call vividly. "Look," he told me. "I'm eighty years old. I've had a happy and productive life. The folks at the hospice where I'm at, here in Washington, have made me very comfortable getting me ready to call it quits. My family are here saying goodbye, and that's why I'm calling you. I'm planning a couple of memorial services and I want you, along with a few others, to speak at both of them: the formal one in Washington and the informal one on the Vineyard. I've decided to go quietly. Happily."

The news was stunning. Mary and I have known and loved the man for over fifty years, admired him. We were fans of his column, his books. If he was difficult or cranky occasionally, well . . . who wasn't?

181

Ninety percent of the time, he was a joy. Ten percent, he was a pain in the ass.

But then came the deluge.

Newspaper articles. Television interviews. Gossip columns that hadn't been paying a lot of attention were now full of news of what he'd decided to do. Old girlfriends were showing up to console him. You've never seen a happier man at death's doorstep.

Suddenly, he began writing his column again for anyone willing to print it. And of course, predictably, book publishers began skulking around, offering him huge advances.

So, he decided that — sure, he'd write that book. Everything but the last chapter, which you're reading now.

The folks who have written for this last chapter were each asked for about a thousand words and to please get it in quickly (no fee, of course) because Random House would like to bring it to the market in time for the Christmas season and make Art (on the *New York Times* bestseller list again) the happiest fraud alive.

By Ben Bradlee

We should have known it was coming, another Buchwald book, and never mind all this stuff about terminal illness. Artie can squeeze a book out of a busy signal.

Close to forty years ago in Paris some creep came into my *Newsweek* office one day with a bandage around his head and bloodstains all over his gabardine suit, claiming to be a deported mobster fresh out of Sing-Sing on a murder rap. His name was Frank Frigenti, and he was after a bunch of French francs. I couldn't get rid of him, no matter how I tried. So I told him to try Buchwald, a couple of floors down, and I figured I'd learn what happened next day when we played an hour or two of gin rummy.

What happened was this: Art sat him down for a couple of hours, fed him once or twice, and interviewed him some more. Got him a hotel room and interviewed him still more. Frigenti got one more night at the hotel, and then a plane ticket to Naples to rejoin his fellow deportees. (Still wearing the bloody suit.)

Artie got $50,000 for a book called *A Gift from the Boys,* which he then sold to the movies (*Surprise Package,* starring Yul Brynner and Mitzi Gaynor) for more thousands.

They got a lot of money for the movie by telling everyone that Cary Grant was interested. He really was, Art says now, but "he didn't like the treatment." Whatever. Big deal!

As you can tell, I admire Art Buchwald. A lot!

In Paris more or less fraudulently after the war on the GI Bill of Rights, Art first caught the world's notice as the Paris *Trib*'s restaurant critic, then as a feature writer about the more or less famous people who went to those restaurants and nightclubs. He made everyone sound interesting and funny, even when they weren't.

I don't think any of us understood how nervous he was about coming back to America, especially to Washington, which he did not know well — to put it charitably. He could have gotten in line behind Leonard Lyons, or Earl Wilson, and achieved unique status that way.

The really great funny men of that time had all gravitated to television: Jack Benny, Fred Allen, Ed Wynn. And Art spotted the slot that he eventually occupied virtually by himself: the man who used humor to place current events in a perspective all his own. Laughing at the man-made predicaments that preoccupied the politicians and voters.

Within a couple of weeks after he and his family settled here in Washington, I brought Art together with another of my best pals, a man named Harry Dalinsky, universally known only as Doc, who ran the Georgetown Pharmacy at the corner of Wisconsin Avenue and O Street. For most of us, Doc was the unofficial mayor of Georgetown, dispensing wisdom, advice, cigars, jokes, psychiatric consultations, and newspapers to his friends and customers from Jack Kennedy on down. When the *New York Herald Tribune* wrote something Kennedy disliked, he officially banned the *Trib* inside the White House, while asking Arthur Schlesinger to pick up the regular White House copies on his way to work every morning for him to read on the Q.T.

Doc and Art became inseparable, and one day I figured out why. Art decided to visit his old man, who was living in Flushing. He wanted company and asked me to come along. We were sitting in some restaurant near the New York airport when this guy shuffles in, the spit and image of Doc. It was Art's dad.

Well, Doc left us some years ago, and now Art is threatening to do the same thing.

Maybe.

Some day.
No hurry, pal.

By George Stevens, Jr.

Mr. President, Laura, Mr. Secretary General, Your Excellencies, members of the Diplomatic Corps, President Chirac, and friends:

I was thinking during the flyover by the Marine Corps Fighter Squadron a few moments ago just how remarkable is the journey of that boy from a foster home in Queens who persevered and made his way to the top of the literary and social scene in the United States. Today he has, as he did so often during his brilliant career, brought America and France closer together and made the world a more loving place.

As everyone here knows, Art was a very modest — yes, we might even say a *humble* man. So he would be surprised that we are gathered here to overflowing in the National Cathedral for his memorial. His humility led him to believe, when he was planning each and every detail of his own memorial service, that all of his friends and admirers would fit into the Washington Hebrew Congregation on Macomb Street. I don't recall ever seeing so many beautiful women at a memorial service as have come here today to honor Art. Your presence brings to mind the words that Art lived by: "The sword is mightier than the pen."

Throughout his life Art shunned the spotlight and was deeply embarrassed by praise and adulation, so I will fulfill his mandate and keep my remarks to just three minutes — an achievement that evaded Art's grasp through a long life of toasts and speeches.

I met Art on a balmy spring evening in 1957. He was sitting on the terrace of the Carlton Hotel on the Croisette during the Cannes Film Festival. The glamorous Greek star Irene Papas was at Art's side. At the next table was the matador Luis Miguel Domínguín. People had faces in those days. Art had placed himself at the center of the European glamor scene, having gained fame for his wry coverage of the Monaco wedding of Princess Grace for the *International Herald Tribune*.

When Art and I shook hands that night, I had no way of knowing that the smiling man with a cigar would bring joy into my life (and into the life of the woman I would later marry) for the next forty-nine years.

All through those years Art's sense of mischief brightened the days of his friends — there was always fun to be had. Whether we were meeting for lunch, for dinner, for tennis, or for a Redskins game, Artie came to play. Ed Wynn, the great comedian from the vaudeville era, used to say that some people had the gift of "thinking funny." Art had that gift.

It was that gift — paired with a keen understanding of human nature — that enabled him to become the brightest writer of American humor of his day. My father, an admirer of the great James Thurber, observed that Buchwald was just as funny as Thurber had been in *The New Yorker,* but Art had to do it three times a week.

And that humor added spice to the lives of his friends. One day during the Jimmy Carter years we were having lunch at the Sans Souci, a small restaurant where all the diners had a view of everyone else. Art spotted Mike Blumenthal dining with Robert McNamara across the room. Blumenthal was Carter's treasury secretary and had launched a crusade against expense account meals, vowing to stop deductions for the "three-martini lunch." Art dispatched a waiter to deliver six martinis to the secretary's table.

In 1967 Bob and Ethel Kennedy gave a seventy-fifth birthday party for Averell Harriman. The guests were asked to come in a costume that represented some phase of Averell's long life. It was Art's idea to go to the Washington wax museum, where we made a deal with the owner. At the climactic moment of the evening Art called for a curtain to be drawn to reveal Averell's friends from World War II, Winston Churchill, Joseph Stalin, and Franklin Roosevelt, seated side by side.

Art presided in full ringmaster's regalia for twenty years as the Master of Ceremonies and chief judge at the Hickory Hill Pet Show for the benefit of Junior Village. He was shameless in awarding prizes to the children of his friends, winning the lasting allegiance of their mothers. And for decades Art could be counted on to dress up as a rabbit each Easter Sunday. During his stay at the Washington Hospice, a long-lost friend sent him an 8-millimeter color film of the 1967 Easter egg hunt at his and Ann's house on Hawthorne Street with vivid images of Robert Kennedy, Walter Lippmann, and David Brinkley talking to the amiable rabbit with horn-rimmed glasses and long bunny ears while youngsters scrambled across the lawn in search of the golden egg. The Easter memories of two generations of Washington children are indelibly tied to Art Buchwald.

And many of those children have Art to thank for getting into the university of their choice. Art would write recommendations describing his friends' children in hilarious letters that somehow made the applicant appear to be an individual of surpassing quality, and gave university presidents the opportunity to boast to friends about the great letter Art Buchwald wrote them. Art claims that no one he recommended was ever rejected.

So, Artie, in the sad times and in the glad times, you were the very best of friends. You brightened our lives and eased our burdens at the same time you were using your unmatched skill as a political humorist to make life miserable for the scoundrels.

It is easy to say this — Artie, you are the very best.

By Ken Starr

Art was family. From the moment I first met him I realized he was a unique human being.

We met when Peter Stone urged Art to have lunch with me (which we did at the Laurent in New York City). I became his "financial guy," as he referred to me, and, eventually, family.

My father and my brothers and I had always read his column, and meeting our household legend was a treat.

If you read Art's column you knew Art, because it reflected his feelings, humor, angst, and very inner being.

He was outraged by injustice, as loyal as any person you could imagine, and as irreverent as we all wish we could be.

He loved life with a passion most of us only dream about. Ann, his children, his friends, and his column were the focal points of his life. His priorities were always right.

He grew up in the Bronx, as I did, and he had that fierce sense of loyalty that most Bronxites have.

He was a Marine, and they gave him a parade which was one of the proudest moments of his life.

He did indeed walk with presidents, kings,

192

and the rich and famous, and never changed who he was; simply, he was Art.

If you knew Art, you met the most interesting people, who all were on a first-name basis with him. Position, fame, or wealth never entered the equation; the most powerful people in every field were merely Pete, Sandy, Ethel, Frank, Barbara, Bill, and on and on.

When Paramount and Art were at the most intense part of the now famous "Buchwald Clause" lawsuit, Marty Davis, then head of Paramount, asked Art to be the key speaker at a charity event where Davis was receiving an award. And as with all his speaking engagements, he was brilliant. His speeches were original, hilarious, and not to be missed. (I should know — one year I told him I would attend all his speeches. I attended many that year, but he gave over thirty.)

At dinner parties, everyone wanted the wit and wisdom of Buchwald, and the choice seats were always the ones to his right and left. Women loved him, and men reveled in his humor and insight.

He touched people's lives by paying for the education of their children, health insurance, vacations, and numerous other gifts merely because he wanted their lives to be better.

He was at our home every Passover, joining in the service with the gusto of a teen-ager.

He was the family photographer, taking pictures constantly, to the extent that my daughters thought Uncle Art was a photographer by profession. When they asked for a picture of him, he sent one taken of him in a bunny suit along with Janet Reno.

We had an almost ritual lunch every month at the Four Seasons Grill Room, which was always a highlight. We discussed everything personal, business, and political; he was always the focal point of everyone there.

Over the years I realized that the most special thing about Art, the thing that could never be replicated, was that he was Art. He was part of our family, but I discovered that he was part of at least a hundred other families. The phrase "Art is family" has been used so often by so many, and it was always true.

So we haven't just lost a writer, a columnist, a man who stood up for all of us, a friend and a confidant, we have lost an integral part of our family. We will miss you, Art, but to paraphrase one of your books: "We will always have you in our hearts."

By Dr. Michael A. Newman

Art was an acquaintance before becoming my patient. Doc Dalinsky introduced me to Art at the Georgetown Pharmacy. Doc was a great character known and special to almost everyone who has spoken today. Doc was Art's surrogate father. A few years later, Art, age fifty-four, and Ann became patients. We were together as patients, friends, and extended family for nearly thirty years. And in a way, Art, who resembled my father, who had died at age fifty-four, became a surrogate father to me.

As a patient, Art was always a challenge. He was pleased to be a poster boy for depression, along with Mike Wallace and Bill Styron. As one of the "blues brothers," he was a great advocate for mental health. He always supported psychotherapy and psychopharmacology; he made referrals and always followed up to see how someone was doing. However, when it came to physical fitness, he was less enthusiastic. In the early 1980s, with other patients, he joined a seven A.M. exercise program at the George Washington University gym. Art was actually working out, getting in shape, and even reluctantly giving up his cigars. Within a few months he looked great, he'd lost weight, and his blood pressure was lower.

But he became profoundly depressed and was hospitalized for several weeks. There were several contributing factors, but as Art explained, "Mike, the fitness program and quitting cigars nearly killed me. Anyway, I figured out that the time I would spend exercising exceeded my increase in life span. It isn't worth it."

Admonitions about diet, exercise, weight, blood pressure, etcetera, were always met with "Aw, I know, I know, but gee, a guy has to have some fun." Going over the results of his physical exam and of various tests, scans, etcetera, I commented that he looked better in person than on paper. His response was, "That's good; that's good." In 2000 he had a stroke, and while hospitalized, developed major medical complications so that for weeks he was critically ill. As is common for patients, he had no recollection of these events, and when later all was recounted to him, his response was, "Well, it sounds interesting, but I'm glad I don't really remember being there." He loved rehab with the attentive nurses, physical therapists, speech therapists, occupational therapists. He worked hard, was always flirtatious, and was always able to make the staff feel good. Of course they loved working with him. This was his modus operandi: to make people laugh, feel good, and like him. It always worked.

These past two years were privately difficult, but publicly he always rose to the occasion. He had a progressive decline in kidney function, and dialysis was anticipated. He agreed, but wanted to spend the summer on Martha's Vineyard with the friends who were his extended family. Medically he always did better on the Vineyard and came home in better shape. This fall [2005] he was preparing to begin dialysis, when he had the acute onset of a circulatory problem in his right leg due to emboli from an aneurysm of the popliteal artery, which eventually necessitated amputation of his right leg below the knee. He was uncertain about having the amputation but understood that dying of a gangrenous leg was not a good option, so that whatever his final decision would be, he should at least begin dialysis and proceed with the surgery. Again, it was his decision, and it was a good decision to proceed, as it enabled Art to have remarkable and extended final weeks with family and friends, colleagues, diplomats, his adoring public, and also recipients of the Art Buchwald Award given to the most irreverent student at the USC School of Journalism. He got letters and calls from around the world, including North Korea!

Dialysis was stopped and Art entered the Washington Home and Hospice. Defying all medical expectations, his condition stabilized and in some ways improved. Again, he looked better in person than on paper. Patients with end stage renal disease are usually on a restricted diet. Abandoning any restrictions, Art ate with enthusiasm — McDonald's breakfasts, blintzes, Reuben sandwiches, cheesecake, lemon pound cake; in effect, anything and everything — and enjoyed it all. The most therapeutic influence was the outpouring of love and attention from all of you here. Every day he would remark about who had visited, called, and written, and who was coming the next day. Medically the last weeks were simply of supportive palliative care by the extraordinary staff of the Washington Home and Hospice. This was the perfect venue for Art's final appearance. What really made a difference was not medical technology or support but rather this tsunami of affection, appreciation, and love whose currents swept across his entire life. The boy from the orphanage, never sure if he would ever be loved, had at the end of his life the certainty of an abundance of love, and he loved this. He was also energized by being able to speak about dying, death, and beliefs about what might happen after death. In his most telling style, poignant and with good humor, he raised the issue and gave it focus. And once again his actions, interviews, and columns had great impact on so many.

When Art died, it was a good death. He was comfortable and understood that in his very good and extraordinary life he had achieved his goal of being loved, and that was the very best therapy.

By Joel Buchwald

We are here to say goodbye to my father, a man who became a living icon in his chosen profession.

He was born to Eastern European immigrants. He was the only boy, the youngest of four children. He never met his mother, and it was only three years ago that for the first time he visited her grave. Dad spent his childhood in foster homes, eventually running away to join the Marines as an underage volunteer during World War II. He did this in part to impress a girl. He never stopped trying to impress girls. The Marine Corps became a home for him. All his life, when he went for a haircut, he wanted a Marine-style haircut — short.

Following the war, he entered USC along with thousands of other newly discharged GIs. When told that he couldn't graduate because he didn't have a high school diploma, he didn't let that stop him from attending classes.

After three years he left for the pleasures of Paris, where he started writing a column for the Paris *Herald Tribune,* and he is still writing his column today. He's been writing his column for over fifty years, and that may qualify him for the Guinness Book of World Records.

In Paris his life changed. He met Ann Mc-Garry. She led him to the altar and made an honest man of him. He and Mom adopted my two sisters, Connie and Jennifer, and me. He was always there for us, and he always provided a home for us. There may have been times when we didn't want to come home, but home was always there if we wanted it.

If I had a problem with something, Dad always taught me to look at it from another point of view. He was never rigid, but fairly lenient and liberal. But he didn't tolerate jackasses.

He started lecturing on college campuses and collecting honorary degrees. He probably received more degrees from more universities than even Billy Graham. It was his way of getting even with the system.

And he became famous — a celebrity. We children grew up on the edge of the spotlight shining on him. People always ask, "What was it like growing up with him? Was he always funny? Did he make you laugh at home?"

The answer is yes, but we had nothing else to compare it with; he was our only father. He used to crack that if the family didn't supply him with one idea a week for his column, we wouldn't get dinner!

A little over thirteen years ago, Mom was diagnosed with lung cancer. Following her death, Dad moved to New York, living on pastries from the local deli.

Then, a few years ago, on Father's Day, he suffered a stroke. He spent that summer in a hospital, completely out of it. Jennifer, Connie, and my girlfriend at the time, Tamara, all took turns watching him in the hospital.

I remember quite clearly coming into the room and holding his hand and talking to him, not knowing if he understood me. His reaction was to grip my hand and to try to pull himself out of bed. He desperately wanted to be out of there. His reaction was characteristic of him. He knew what he wanted and he wasn't going to stop trying for it. He was fighting for his life, and he never stopped fighting.

This was an important lesson for me. Even today, when I think about it, I can still feel the strength and intensity of his grip, squeezing my hand.

After his rehab, we decided that Dad would come and live temporarily with Tamara and me until we knew what shape he was going to be in, and what he might want for himself. He never left us. When Tamara and I married, Dad was the best man.

Our house filled up nicely with two grand-children, Corbin and Tate. Their grand-father was there for them, and he loved them, the way we always loved him.

By Jennifer Buchwald

I know Dad wants us to celebrate and laugh, so here goes, Daddio.

Dad called me up on July 10.

"Hi, Jenny," he woke me up with. "I want you to send me your eulogy a.s.a.p. so it can get put in my book."

"My what?" I replied, not knowing if this was a dream or not.

"I talked to you about this."

"When, Dad? This is the first I've heard of this. What's the plan?"

"Shit, didn't you get the e-mail from Cathy explaining it all?"

"No, Dad. Is this when you told me? In her e-mail?"

"Shit, I will have her send it again."

"Dad, can you explain what you are doing? You are not dead yet."

"Well, I am putting my funeral in my book, so the publisher needs your paper now. Everyone else has theirs in, like Mike Wallace, Tom Brokaw, and Ben Bradlee."

"Well, Dad, obviously my life is much busier than theirs, and my secretary is on vacation. But don't you think this is weird, Dad? This should be an *elegy*."

"A what?"

"An elegy is how you honor someone when they are alive, and then there is the *eulogy* that is written to celebrate someone after they die."

"No, you just don't get it. Just write it by tomorrow and send it in. My publisher is waiting."

"So, Dad, what tense do I use?"

"Hell if I know. Love you. Bye."

Then I called Mike Wallace to see what he thought. His response was the same as so many responses all my life about Dad. "Well, if Artie asks for something, I do it for him, because he is Artie."

That was enough for me to get to my computer and write this eulogy for my dad.

My Fellow Americans.

I think he deserves those three words to be a Buchwaldism in the Big Book of Isms. Those three words have made millions laugh. I loved to hear everyone laugh and watch his response. He was so excited and totally joyful laughing along with them at his jokes. Going to his speeches warmed my insides and made me so proud of having a dad who had such a healing and healthy and honest job. Oh, yes, also having a father with a very unique sense of humor. When Dad got put in hospice, we all believed that it was a one-way trip. Magically, he got a round-trip ticket with frequent flyer miles! No one expected this. He is now collecting on all his miles to see how far he can go.

This has been such a unique situation for Dad. He was able to decide between living and dying. Not many have that choice. He chose death when he thought that was the way he was headed, back in January. As you probably know, my dad almost went into the light, but only the good die young, and Darwin was right — Dad's a living example of survival of the fittest . . . and funniest! Obviously, a higher power has an alternate plan for him. Dad has more laughs to share with everyone before he leaves.

We are all so excited with how happy and full of life he is. It's such a joy to see Dad so content. He came to terms with his own death, which most never get a chance to do. He is very happy and at peace with his decision to die and with death whenever that happens, and in the meantime he's extremely happy with his extended lifetime. Dad's four big passions are food, being center stage, spending time with friends, and writing. Remember the magical tunnel from the hospice directly to McDonald's? When they heard of this, they offered to deliver his food, with no delivery charge.

I have always known Dad to be center stage. What an incredible presence and talent and love of making people laugh. Being with him off and on for four months when he was in hospice, I saw how loved he is all over the world. Some people came in to meet him who didn't even know him. He is so interested in everyone's stories, rich or not. Back in March, Mike Wallace — and only Mike would or could do this — called Dad up one day and said, "Okay, Artie, cut the crap, we know you aren't sick. You've had enough attention to last you two more lifetimes. And all the awards you have received while in hospice have proven you will die with the most awards. Not to mention all the interviews you have done on national TV and talk shows. You even made it into *People* magazine!! What else do you want? It's time to get your butt out of that bed and come back to your computer. Enough talk — start typing."

Dad called his administrative and life assistant Cathy Crary and dictated his first article.

Welcome back, Dad.

Next came Thursday's column, just in time to document our president's drop below 30 percent approval rating — a joy for any political humorist.

Dad gave me so many gifts in life. Of course there were the material ones that we got in abundance. But it is the ones that I don't need to carry but I have them with me always that are the priceless ones. The good memories I remember in Paris. Riding the carousels, and being so short I had to walk on my tippy-toes to hold Dad's hand on our many walks for ice cream. Then in America I loved to be with him when he was silly wearing those funny costumes. I loved him putting me to sleep making up stories for me every night. Dad is deaf in his right ear, and me in my left. When we would walk on each other's deaf sides, it took about five minutes to realize we had two completely separate conversations going on. What else could we do but laugh?

He was there during the tumultuous times too, and there were many. Once he even flew back from France because he heard I needed him. I learned early that when I'd ask Mom for something and she would usually say no, that I could always count on Dad to say yes. It was also the little things that meant the most. Like letting us have our talent show at our house when I was about nine, despite my going out and selling tickets to all the neighbors. When they arrived, there wasn't enough sitting room. But the show was horribly successful. Adults are so kind sometimes.

This is another incident that could only

have happened between Dad and me. I was turning onto Main Street in Vineyard Haven with about fifteen other women motorcycle friends. I saw a group of people walking along the sidewalk at the corner. They all stopped to look at us; a few looked scared. I screamed, "Hi, Dad!" He smiled and all his friends clapped and waved us on.

When I chose Dad to be the first one to talk to about being a lesbian, I never feared that he would judge or reject me. He responded in a matter-of-fact voice, as if I had said "Pass the butter, please." "This is just a phase," he said, with all his love.

Whenever Dad was in Boston, he invited me and a few biker friends to have dinner at fancy restaurants with him. Twelve of us would walk into the restaurant with our helmets and all our gear, and the maître d' would be beside himself. Dad would just laugh each time. We were given a whole round table. We weren't allowed to put anything on it, so we loaded our gear on the chairs and under the table. The maître d' then put RESERVED on the table.

I remember Dad and Mom and I tried to stop smoking together. Dad and I were successful. That wrecked his image. Eventually he had to update his photo for his column and it was a big controversy — cigar or no cigar. He chose the new him, yet still today people say to me, "Oh, yeah, he's the one with the cigar." Dad has always had humor in every cell of his body. One day he met a woman I was dating and he said to me, "It won't last. She doesn't laugh." He was right.

When Dad was in China twenty-five years ago, he sent me a postcard saying, "All the women are barefooted and collect rice for 15 hours a day seven days a week. I think you'd love it here. Love, Daddio."

Just the other day I was speaking to Dad about a new surgery for my deaf ear. He said, "Good, get it fixed so you can hear what a pain in the butt you've been for the past forty-nine years."

I asked Dad these questions when he announced around Christmastime that he was choosing to die instead of doing dialysis:

ME: Our family is still very dysfunctional. Have you thought about sticking around to fix us?

DAD (looking over at me with a smile and without hesitation): No.

ME: What will you miss the most when you die?

DAD: My grandchildren.

When I was ten, Dad got a phone call early one Sunday morning from the police department. I had gotten arrested for hitch-hiking. Okay, I might have been a handful, but my point is, I always knew he loved me, or I wouldn't have told the officer my name to begin with.

When I was very young, Dad and I would go on Thanksgiving and Christmas to a soup kitchen to help serve the guests. Those two days a year have turned into many months a year of giving for me. Dad taught me that jokes that hurt people aren't funny (unless it's about a politician). A parent's duty is to make sure all the kids are doing well, especially for a Jewish dad. To most that means marriage. Well, he sure did an excellent job on that duty, setting me up on a blind date. We met and immediately fell in love, and Dad had a beautiful wedding for us on the Vineyard and another amazing daughter-in-law joined our family.

I want to thank all his friends who kept coming to visit Dad at the hospice and wouldn't let go. All the love you brought in thousands of ways fed his spirit and helped heal his body and gave him more mileage. Special thanks to all the different lipsticks that kissed Dad's head until it got so shiny we thought he was going to turn into a Buddha. Ethel Kennedy, your daily anticipated visits gave Dad a reason to wake up each morning. And thank you so much to Eunice Shriver, who stayed in the present with her faith and wouldn't listen to a word of his death talk. Eunice is one of the few people I have ever met (besides Mike Wallace) who can get my dad to shut up and listen to her.

I am so lucky to have been adopted sight unseen and sex unknown by this wonderful man whom I love so much. Dad as a father and a gift giver showed me the importance and power of laughter, and the value of talking to strangers, for we all have stories to tell. I love him for his open acceptance of diversity and of the different ways families can be defined and for his amazing thoughtfulness and willingness to give to others. He taught me the importance of friendship, of using the bathroom every chance you get when traveling, of silliness, of enjoying creamy foods like ice cream every day, of being adventuresome in life, and of kindness.

I am sure right now Dad is holding court with all his angel friends. But today is different. It is his turn to listen. He will laugh and cry along with us as we celebrate his rich and wonderful life.

Dad, you know I will miss you on this earth, but I will carry your laughter and love and gifts forever in my heart. I love you, Dad. Make them laugh in heaven.

When everyone thought I was bound for heaven, Carly Simon said she would sing a song at my memorial service. Then, when it turned out I didn't die, she wrote a song to celebrate my still being here.

**Too Soon to Say Goodbye
by Carly Simon**

> FOR ART BUCHWALD
> LOVE FROM CARLY
> AUGUST 10, 2006

Too soon to say goodbye, my dear
Too soon to let you go
Too soon to say *"Auf Wiedersehen"*
"Au revoir," no no

Too soon to say goodbye, my dear
Too soon to rest my case
Too soon to start another journey
When we've just won the race

Not while the lanterns and chandeliers
Sway in the pale moonlight
Not while the shimmer of far and near
Holds us both so tight

Too soon to say goodbye, my dear
Too soon the tide will rise

But not 'til it reaches another shore
Will I ever say goodbye

Not while the music and fireworks
Sing down the hill to the sound
Not while girls in their summer gowns
Are dancing round and round

Too soon to see the world beyond
I'm willing to be late
Let's stay right here beneath the stars
Let the voyage wait

For it's too soon,
Too soon, to say goodbye
Too soon
To say . . . goodbye.

ABOUT THE AUTHOR

Art Buchwald was born in Mount Vernon, New York, and raised in Hollis, Queens. After serving as a Marine in the Pacific during World War II and attending the University of Southern California, Buchwald left the United States for Paris. There he landed a job with *Variety* magazine and began writing his now-legendary columns, syndicated for decades in more than five hundred newspapers. He received the Pulitzer Prize for Outstanding Commentary in 1982 and was elected to the American Academy of Arts and Letters in 1986. He is the author of thirty-five books, including the *New York Times* bestseller *Leaving Home* and the recent collection of political commentary *Beating Around the Bush*. Art Buchwald died in January 2007.

The employees of Thorndike Press hope you have enjoyed this Large Print book. All our Thorndike and Wheeler Large Print titles are designed for easy reading, and all our books are made to last. Other Thorndike Press Large Print books are available at your library, through selected bookstores, or directly from us.

For information about titles, please call:
(800) 223-1244

or visit our Web site at:
www.gale.com/thorndike
www.gale.com/wheeler

To share your comments, please write:
Publisher
Thorndike Press
295 Kennedy Memorial Drive
Waterville, ME 04901